LOVE NOTES FROM HUMANITY

The Lust, Love & Lost Collection

A FeminineCollective.com Anthology

Published by:
Feminine Collective Media

This is a work of fiction. Names, characters, businesses, places, events and incidents are either the products of the author's imagination or used in a fictitious manner. Any resemblance to actual persons, living or dead, or actual events is purely coincidental.

Copyright © 2017 by Feminine Collective Media

Library of Congress Control Number: 2017902097

Editor: Julie Anderson
Cover and Interior Design: SA Smith
Cover Photo: © 2017 Julie Anderson All Rights Reserved

All Rights Reserved. No part of this publication may be reproduced, stored in a retrieval system, or transmitted, in any form or in any means – by electronic, mechanical, photocopying, recording or otherwise – without prior written permission. Additional copyrights per poem in back of book.

CONTENTS

**FOREWORD BY
JULIE ANDERSON**

LUST - 1
LOVE - 35
LOSS - 77

AUTHOR BIOGRAPHIES - 151

"Nobody has ever measured,
not even poets,
how much the heart can hold."
— **Zelda Fitzgerald**

Love.

It's the complex chemistry of a blind heart and a dreamy mind.

Love is a shapeshifter. Love walks along the same path as hate. Love makes us whole. Love makes us weak. Love drives us to insanity. Love can be a curse. Love is a m racle. Love is a universal language.

This collection of poems takes the reader on a journey through the complexities of that simple four letter word. Curated by FeminineCollective.com, many from this collection have been published on the site since its beginning. Others you will read are new pieces that were written just for this collection.

The writers of these poems are award-winning Authors, Journalists, Bloggers and Activists, while others are previously unknown artists. The voices of the forty-four contributors are diverse. The poems are a collective made from a global community. The authors are from Australia, Canada, Central America, The United Kingdom, The United Arab Emirates, Pakistan, South Africa and The United States.

Written by women and men, between the ages of fifteen and seventy, each poem is unique in every respect. They are raw and unfiltered accounts of each poet's feelings regarding, the love of a child, the loss of a family member, sex, dating, marriage, divorce and finding love for one's self.

I believe that every one of the writers and the words that they are willing to share with you, dear reader, are a gift for all of humanity.

May you always know and feel loved,

Julie Anderson

Publisher, Feminine Collective

LUST

Love Notes From Humanity

Seductress of Sin - Julie Anderson

A heretic grin
interlaced with longing.
Ferocious need danced behind barren eyes.
Her poise.
Thunder clouds and electricity,
lead me to believe in her gospel of sin.

Where it not for her blithe commentary,
fornicating in the sea,
under stars,
against incidental walls,
I might not have chosen this bestial path.

Eyes shut.
Mouth taste free.
Skin cracking, lacking soothing lubricant.

Verbs worked their magic,
I performed, as she suggested.

Hinted
Sighed
Proposed

Burning vowels propelled each thrust.
Sinner who was a Saint.

Worshiping
Idolizing
Fondling

Physical glory.
Hedonistic behavior my own.
Pleasure points of deception,
etched into the surface of time.

Seeing
Sensing
Seducing

My quest for consumption continues,
unabated.
Demons laugh.
The devil delights.

Flesh burns bright,
smells spent.
Tastes salty with a tang of regret.

Hell is on Earth,
Mistress of ceremonies,
some say that I am wicked.

Love Stinks - Jacqueline Cioffa

The steam rolls off her back
And down her freshly waxed
Bits and pieces
Exhausting is the pretty prep and fancy

Expensive Italian lace panties
La Perla
Purchased with her own dollars and sweat
Fit snug and smug against her bottom
She is manicured, pedicured, and tweezed

Ready to meet her lover around whatever corner
For a quickie at noon, dusk rendezvous or even the longing midnight hours
He comes to her, unpredictable
She goes to him, uncertain

She smells like fig, delicious
Wearing his favorite scent
He smells clean and dangerous

Too foreign
For old friends with dirty, sexy, new benefits
Hush now
Let's keep this between us
He says
This what? This why? This when?

The *SEX*

Ooooh, that game never ends

She feels all the feels
The vibration, tongue and groove
And yet, she holds back

Insecure, feeling unsafe
In his bed

She can't pee in his house
Weirdo, uncomfortable in her skin
Secret lovers, he whispers out and about
Her body shivers, masking the truth
So much better as friends

Who is this girl?

She doesn't recognize the supple breasts, burgundy nails,
heels, and naked, tight muscles on full display
Her nudity stinks, lovers indifferent
She prefers boy shorts and wears pajama bottoms to bed
If she can't open her heart, she can't taste pleasure on her
mouth

Holding her piss, until bladder affliction
She sweats, fevered, ill and nauseated in his bed
He wakes from the wet pillow casing

Wiping her forehead with a damp cloth of concern
He gently dresses her in the dark
Delirious, she places her arms tight around his waist
Resting her head in the crook of his neck
Cruising on his motorbike feels real and precious

The mist and fog of the empty, forlorn city night
Reeks something like love
The blinking neon sign, 'All Night Pharmacy'
Spells relief
Making the dampness and frigidity in her bones
Feel Intimate

Fig, she breathes in deep his scent
Lingering
He loves her, like a concerned friend

Years later
She never knew if she loved him
Any more or less

Secret lovers disappearing back
Inside the easy, loving, laughter of the good old days, months and years
Time spent together
So much better as friends

Still, and long after
She wears his scent
Claiming it for her very own

Dreams – John Michael Antonio

after all this time
 you are so close
 I could reach out
 and taste you
 but I hover and hesitate
because I want to savor
and devour the moment
bask in the
the heat that emanates
from your core
hear the heaving
breaths of anticipation
see the soft
gyrations of hope
smell the glorious
fragrance of affection
feel the sweet miracle of
your existence
dive into you
kneel at your altar
and kiss your
delicious lips forever

Eden's Palpitation - C. Streetlights

The heart beats
in its own mysterious rhythm
and
without breaking its pattern.

       Until one day it skips.
       (Just like that, it skips.)

Skip. And skips.

The world around us
spins in a new revolution
around a different axis
and
soon a mystery unfolds.

Breaths are taken
and
breaths are held.

Time stands still
and
time flies by.

A possible endless fascination palpitates.

To Kiss a Married Man - Sandy Coomer

it would be
because he was a player
a rake, and we both knew
we were shooting hell
blinded by the way night rolls
he would take his jacket off
his hands on my shoulders
and then my hips, and he
would smell like cognac
and sweet tobacco, his
eyelashes a sweep of shade
against his eyes
blue – no, brown –
dark, carnal, like a leopard
or a lynx, and he would make
no sound and I would hate him
hate his silence, hate
knowing he could take
this kiss, so sure
the night would hide us
the light a subtle arc reaching
but not finding
knowing I was one
of many, thinking him
weak, indifferent
I could be unfeeling too
the watching of him leaving
bringing
no anxious rise of longing
no pain, no ache in my chest
no catch that brings a gasp
wrecking the morning
it would be that
only that, so it could never
not ever, be you.

Mistress Desire and the Lonely Flame - Clementine Heath

And then at once she understood.
Through the veil of denial she so cleverly disguised herself,
never to question, never to explore and always to deny.
The biggest sacrifice of all,
her vulnerability.
Locked away,
removing any threat of emotion or feelings beyond her control,
in aid to her constitution,
her obedience and duty.
There would be no room for Ecstasy.
Not hers alone.
She was a giver, not a receiver.
Numb to her own gifts.
She was void of all that which she so cleverly created in this role-play world of Suits and Slaves and Misbehaves.
And in this moment...this unprepared immediate moment,
the veil was lifted.
Her cage: Broken.
And a wave of emotion flooded her veins and fi led her entire being with a sensation,
unlike anything she could have ever comprehended possible.
Never to be the same again.
She now understood what it was all about.
And she wanted more...

The Descent - Clementine Heath

Mistress Desire
Beyond simple truth.
Beyond the reaches of words and description.
Lust and danger at the hand of this Tall Dark Stranger.

His drug worked quickly.
Sex kisses
He stamped his impression hard.
A strong tongue
he kissed with purpose.

Her heart skipped beats racing to catch up to itself,
Only to lose breath and motion
And her conscious awareness.
Trembling desperately within, urges buried deep.

Her body could not contain itself.
Flooding her amorous sack of Lust's Venus Cave
The storm was heavy and fierce,
The numbing coma now washed away.

Hot flushes burning soft cheeks.
A sting so familiar but this time it was pleasure,
Uncontrollable.
She was changed... revived.

It was not out of choice but necessity.
All these years she had betrayed herself,
All these years in the darkness of denial and servitude.
The starving beast now had a taste for the blood of it

The elixir of life breathed heavily into her heart.
The lonely flame danced feverishly with the new cosmic wave.
So enthused by this enchanting delight there was no more melancholy here.
But the hunger for more was overwhelming.

The power of it
Murderously consuming.
He aroused something in her...
The beast within was now wide awake.

Disintegration - Clementine Heath

In her darkest hour, she offered herself to Him,
Relinquishing all control.
And He devoured all that she was...
This was not about Love.

Submission was not freedom's choice in the end.She was in
His world now.
Betrayed by her compulsion,
Sanity disintegrated.

Fallen between the cracks,
Leaving only his poisonous token.
He cruelly abandoned her there,
Faded and fractured by cunning persuasion.

Torn inside out,
His venom raged inside her like a plague
He, the stranger with the key:
This serpent, this wolf - poisonous prick.

Urges desperately run from,
Now a numbing obsession.
Beyond reason or logic,
There could be no substitute now.

Reflections of Innocence betrayed,
Her thoughts haunted by the trick of it.
And the shame grew more powerful burning for it...
She spread herself thin.

Bitterness beneath the clouds of a new day,
Comatose the days away.
Twisted thoughts,
The highway to calamity was close at hand.

Enslaved, she longed to feel alive again.
A simple seduction...
Lust's evil trick.

Oh, the Fuckery!

Absolution - Clementine Heath

Emotions methylated,
Her dreams syncopated.
Quietened by the slumber,
A virgin flame burns.

And then at once she understood…

Through the veil of denial she had betrayed herself.
Beyond the reaches of her sanity,
Drowned out the girl she once knew.

Awakened from the melancholy madness,
A constant whisper delivers solace
Violating her cells with Mercy.
There is no room in her soul for the Servitude after all.

The longing washed away.
This slightly creature shed her skin,
Transformed.
Enchanted no more by the Mistress.

She crawled her way back to the surface.
Shimmering speckles disturb a ghostly haze.
Enraptured by Spring's morning song,
She breathed in the savageness of the dew.

Thawed.
Such delicate beauty in the fractures.
Releasing from within her
The last dying breath of old… Primal Screams.

Simple silver, sharper than the prick!
Tattooed her naked flesh.
Lessons learned carved deep into her canvas,
Necessary truths.

A distant cry in the wind wails familiar echoes.
Once haunted by these stray howls,
Now a soothing lullaby.
And so the Beast was laid to rest.

Buried along with the torment of It,
The memory of what never was and will never be.
And in this moment,
This unprepared immediate moment…

She was free

An Abyss - Margret Avery

The blood in my veins
holds him like that
last drop of wine
you will never taste
again. ...

For his illness seeped
into an abyss that I
will never see how it
all began

circling
spiraling
signaling
all my
weakness
for love
unbridled
untitled
separate
& together
melding
into each
other
without
the thunder
of angst
only the
peace of
each other

in a
world
unknown
to anyone
who doesn't
see the
chord
that locks
our need
to not
produce
a seed.

Stuck Inside - H.M. Jones

Press your tongue
the red center of me
feel you satiate
my entirety.

Moan you in,
push you out
of my confidence.
Feel you swell
under my imagination;
you are unreal,
my perfect creation.

Dreaming up reality
you are firmly stuck
inside of me.

Why Men Secretly Fear Women - John Michael Antonio

naked before me
your body
and
my fears
as your touch delivers
me to you
unleashing an animal passion
that engulfs
and
inspires
the stirring
and
my whispering
of the words of eternity
as your smiling eyes
brush aside
my terror
and
boyish posturings
and
I clandestinely
surrender
to the onslaught of
your sweet awesome power
now and forever

Carnal Dream - Julie Anderson

Don't say a word
Let me feel you
smell you
know your secrets
savor the aftermath

Floating in and out
flesh
decadent fantasy
warm breath
strong hands

hold me
the weight of my being
let me rest under your chin
above your heart

perfection
caress me on fire
your fingers
only in dreams

lucid thought
deja vu
Hot flashing strikes
ignite curiosity
endless possibility

Play here with me
in between consciousness
and death
dark velvet night
we have a moonless sky

time does not exist

I feel you
I taste you
I think you
Real

I want more

Once - Sandy Coomer

This game, and I should say
a name is what I want
a fact to hold against
the things we do -
nineteen minutes on the train
between Montrose and Grand
every one of them burning
with your gaze, my
shoulder blades melting, my hips
my neck, my open mouth
your hair disheveled, your jeans
lazy on lean legs
three seats away, even here
your eyes are deep
your hands
wide reaching. Once
mechanics hovered at the engine
the too-soon repair
a gift of a dozen rounds of time
you smiled, shrugged
I felt the need to moan
you twisted your ring
I covered mine
one person between us
two steps away, your arm
on the rail – your fingers
against the seat
stretching, fumbling.
I know you, don't know you.
I only want to touch you once.

It Happened Under the Electric Sky - Peter Olson

He moves around the humanity.
Throughout the sea of neon hula hoops and pony beads
The laser beams and sparkly strobe lights
Trying to find his friends he came with that night.

The beats are infectious and the vibes are sublime.
And that's when he sees her.

Green draped hoodie top.
Sequined green metallic bottoms.
Kandi bracelets adorn her arms

Her body moves in time to the beat
Her soul moves to the rhythm

Her skin sparkles as the lights
and the lasers
and strobe lights
bounce from every bead of sweat
and every piece of glitter
pinned to her body.

She glances around and look at him.
They lock eyes as she wryly smiles at him.
She knows he's there as she closes her eyes.
She lets the music consume her.

The music moves her body,
as she its willing muse.

She slowly lick her lips
and sensually bites the edge of her lip.
Thinking of him,
moving his hands down her glistening torso.
Wanting to feel him touch her.
She turns around and reaches out toward him.
She looks at him and slowly removes her hood.
She seductively smiles and pulls him close.

She whispers in his ear...

"There's nothing sexier than dancing close to someone to a hard-driving techno beat."

She moves her cheek across his face to his lips.
Her hand tenderly careering his face.
And she kisses him.

They smile at each other as beat goes on
Dancing close to one another.

Touching each other.
Holding each other.
Becoming one with the music.

She turns around and they kiss again.
She whispers in his ear...
"I'm yours tonight if you'll have me."

"Yes. Off course," he says
In his mind,
"Yes, my love...a million times yes."
But he's paralyzed.

He's memorized.
He can't speak.
He can't think.
He can't answer back.

She kisses him again
Slowly moving her hand down his right arm.
Interlocking fingers,
she moves his hand
around to her lower back.

She whispers in his ear...

"Please give me a chance.
Please let us have just this one last dance."

He's dumfounded.
He's spellbound.
He's memorized.

She giggles mischievously.

"I knew it," she says. "You ARE perfect."

She takes two steps toward him, caressing his cheek...
...and kisses him one last time.

Lustfully. Passionately.

She whispers to him...
"I should have been, baby...
I could have been yours."

She turns around away from him.
Slowly,
covering her head with
her green draped hood.
With both arms reached high,
one arm sensually moving
down the other.

Her body moves in time to the beat
Her soul moves to the rhythm.

And in the sea of neon hula hoops and pony beads
She disappears.
She disappears into the never after.

He continues to stare for her through the sea of humanity.
But he's paralyzed.

Watching her walk away.

Gardening Tip - Susan P. Blevins

Our eyes locked across the cocktail lounge
First sparks
I held her gaze, daring her resistance

We crossed the room and talked
Discovered things in common,
mostly magnetic physical attraction
Naked flames

We met for coffee
Fire was fed
Went to her place
Conflagration

She came to my place
Allergic to my cats
Well, love me, love my cats
Flames lacked oxygen

A rendezvous postponed
A headache
Love died as fast as it had started
Cold ashes all that's left

Good for my rose garden

On Chapin Street - Nan Byrne

We sat bare assed and wetting our hunger condensing. In a cloud of Jack Daniels you dealt a final round. Drawing each card slowly from the deck, fingers placed like a gentle lover between the folds of the cut. Lifting each card into the growing fan of your hand, you laughed then knocked the deck roughly with your knucklebone for my turn. Snapped out my five little fishes with their milk bellies up. The short parade of twos, the comical pair of Jack and Queen, a three. You offered your spades from their black hole, and I understood nothing in the soft spread of the numbers would keep me from my knees   So, I went down with you behind, two dogs burying the same bone. Thinking I might love you, thinking I might want to die this way or live this way always—smelling the stink of a day burning out on Chapin Street.

Every Other Thursday -
Elizabeth Kirkpatrick Vrenios

I

We meet,
and I dash across the room
at his knock, to open
and feel the heat of his body
engulf me like a blaze in my own galaxy.
He runs his rough tongue
over my salty skin
all of its parts, sunburnt and scarred,
and I crackle and burn,
the shock runs through me
like power to our bedside lamp.

Full orb of my body
curves and glows
arcs over and over the afternoon
in our roadside room,
deep in a universe of two,
curtains drawn,
glasses empty on the sink, bare,
unwrapped.

I trace the angles of his face
to gently call him up from sleep
and hope he will wake to begin again.

The incandescent sphere outside our window,
casts a glow through the curtain,
a moon we have made our own.

II

Year after year,
there is the same room,
the same click of a key,
the same tumblers wrapped in waxy paper,
blinds drawn.

My ear, a shell-print tattooed on his shoulder
brands him mine as he sleeps.
Half-awake I dream of a future,
while unspoken words eat away
at an eroding shore
pounded by the sea.
He murmurs from a faraway island,
behind a barricade I cannot touch

I love you

as I wait...
as I wait...
and watch the motel's plastic ball,
blink on
blink off.

III

On our last Thursday
a shiver breaks through the surface
of our silence
like unwelcome sunlight bruising the air.
You know, I hate my wife and never speak to her,

and I cringe, as I imagine her depth of loneliness,
a life dried up like a splatter
on the linoleum floor.

I no longer recognize his mouth
or the flesh of his belly,
the years worn down
to reveal their truth. Accustomed
to stroking his back,
my fingers lock themselves inside
their caged fists. I turn my head away.

Outside, the neon moon buzzes
sour and pungent,
the clock hums with its own dim circular story
not quite keeping the hour,

and for the first time
I notice
the small exit door sign:
How to escape
in case of fire.

Guilty Pleasures - John Michael Antonio

those defiant nights
the flowers of our imagination
dripping with life
the lights of the steel
and glass jungle
shining auspiciously for us
reaching for your hand
and you reaching back
knowing their machinations
and judgments
were powerless against
our racing and fearless hearts

All I Ask - Dori Owen

I told you once
a long
time ago.
Truth be told
I've told
you
so many times.
Stay away.
Keep your distance.
You know the
consequences
of getting
too close.
I run, yet
you wonder why.
And so it goes.
If you only knew
what I could
give
if I felt free.
Unrestrained.
I'm insatiable.
But there is
a price.
Stay away.
Keep your distance.
I can promise you
a paradise
you've never
known.
But I
must be free.
Not owned.
I can take you
to the
valley of the gods.
And beg for more.

But all I ask is
Stay away.
Keep your distance.
You called me
uncontainable
and I
thought
for one moment
you understood.
But I was wrong.
You didn't stay away.
You didn't keep distance.
Don't feel
alone.
There will be
more.
And each time
I'll tell them
if you want me
Stay away.
Keep your distance.
One more time.

Sex with Strangers - Julie Anderson

It was a dare, oh yes it was
I was young
crazy
and in lust.

You were dangerous.
The right kind of madness
had arrived just in time.

We were in the city,
the one where anything goes
where no one tells
private
secrets
laced with lies.

Your lack of experience
intoxicated me.
I had been thinking about it,
during lonely nights
in foreign hotel rooms.

How easy it would be
to dial the number.

Uncomfortable silence not necessary,
a professional knows how to bring forth
locked away fantasies.

Anything you want,
of course only for you.

The dare, I spoke it.
Did it.
Regretted it.

Different places,
I felt evil
and sick.
Never enough,
not for you.

It is your job to keep me happy.
When you are crazy,
it turns me on.

On and on
No secrets
no lies,
unforgettable moments,
third degree burns of shame.

Dirty little liar,
everyone was game.

Just one more time?
Come on, for me?

It is my fantasy; you are the one
who showed me,
I do not want to quit.

It's like having the same meal every single night.
The same flavor every day,
gets boring.
You need to spice it up.
Will you do it, one more time,
please?

Sex with strangers?
Yes,
but this time,
there will be secrets and lies.
The flavor,
I will taste alone.

Love Notes From Humanity

LOVE

Love Notes From Humanity

You Are Star Stuff – SA Smith

Fatally and flawed, beautifully and broken.
Every step you take, every thought you think is a miracle in itself.
Do you have any idea how miraculous it is that you are even here?
So many wish they could be where you are? Doing what you do?
Do you know how many people have come before you, how many generations of you it has taken to get to who you are right now?
You have worked your whole life to be at just this moment.
You are star stuff, baby. Plain and simple.
Hurdling through space at a thousand miles an hour on our little planet we call earth.
Just that alone makes you a miracle, but you have so much more to do.
So many places to go, so many people to see.
Your journey has just begun, no matter how long it may seem to you. You are just beginning.
Each day, one step closer to completing the task
– completing you.
You are growing, learning and taking your first steps into the mystery we call life.
Grab hold, embrace it.
Look around and really see who you are.
Your eyes, finally wide open to the possibilities of you.

You are a miracle.

You are star stuff.

You. Are. Love.

Eleven - Jessica Rinker

Standing here
in the doorway.
I hold my daughter close. She is incandescent;
I move to catch her, to absorb her before she is gone.
Her body incipient, delicate places I've embraced and loathed
the same. She is the sunrise,
the before
on the cusp of everything
that is after
eleven.

To hold my sons
is to love my husband, my father,
but to hold my daughter is to love myself; an eclipse.
In this moment, in this aurora, I'm holding myself, as we two
become three.
myself, as we two become three.
My mother becomes me.
And we are all standing
in the light
of
eleven.

Daughter – Julie Anderson

Light shines from your eyes
Hang on tight
Some will try to plunder the beauty of your soul
Listen to me, I know
They will lie, they always do
Trust your premonition
Do not give yourself away
You are precious and unique
Tell them to leave
The ones whose intentions are selfish
Words will be whispered you dream are genuine
Hang on tight
Do not let go of you
Reflect on your gifts
Own and control
Fight off temptation, don't give in
Who are you?
My one and only
Your one and only
Beloved you.

Bergamot - Tennessee Hill

Our girl was seventeen, and she didn't think
we knew what that meant. The space between us
and our girl is bridged by stories that feel like
figments, to her they are not who we are.
It is a dangerous thing to play, hopscotch across
the lines that gate us into these suburbs. Our girl
was going to the boy's house, the one she loved,
and she thought my cheeks didn't still have holes
from biting away the giggles, that I had never been
the girl she was. The boy was not you but he was close
and that scared you and all your daddy parts. When
our girl came home with a red patch on her wrist,
I felt the heart we share speed up on your side. She
lifted it to my nose and told me to smell, so I sniffed
our girl's red skin and it smelled of London. You
smelled her too as she told us how the boy burned her
on accident, that he dropped a candle and the wax
dripped. It would scar her, you said, and she remembered
in the seventeen year old thoughts I passed down to her,
the night I chipped my tooth on your bourbon glass when
we were undergraduate students drunk on something else.
My boy, the one you still keep, broke me with crystal
and our girl's burned her with a candle that smelled
of Earl Gray and Bergamot and a place she'd never been to.

High School Teen Age Dreams - Elizabeth Regen

So, it's 1992 and I was thinking about you
as I lined the last of my lid -
put my hoop earrings on,
shouldered the Jansport -
I'm gone ---
way before Paris, my tiny white dog's name was Kid.

My hair is all crunchy, wet, long and curly ...
pulled back and snapped in a clip.
My Nautica's red and a little too long - but it's all good
these visuals ... they work for my song ...

I sip a Snapple and don't eat apples but a bag of chips will
do, and here comes that bagel, nice and warm to our table -
it's me and my owls - we're a crew.

It's a Galaxy of fries on the Ave. of 8th - and nothin' cost
more than 5 dollars. Hoots and Hollas, no one reads the
thermometer - it's hot in this bitch --- we relate.

17 and a year is forever - still together and always will be -
not a thought on our minds as we converse and we dine over
this universal high school teenage dream.

Wondering what will come next, but not really carin' - we're
so rich with our time it's disgustin'. We're so new to this
world, we're so young to this place - the way we spend time
... it's a total disgrace ... throwin' hours in the carbage.
puttin' days straight to sleep - weeks disappear in a flash-

another pocket of cash and a month tossed to laughs and
then there's all the up-coming seasons to think ...

we would regulate, and speculate ... who would we marry
and when? would we have boys or girls? let's talk about this
again ... one two or three? who would go first ... you, her or
me?

Not that long ago, just like yesterday, hours ago it seems ...
these hypothetical futures, these sketched out adulthoods,
these universal high school teenage dreams ...

Now it's 16 years later and I saw you today
and those babies are oh so real -
it's like they were there with us -
listenin' in on us
takin' notes as we discussed
they instinctively - just knew the deal.

they were already on their way, their journey had begun ...
long before we even graduated - and in all these things I've
stated, no matter how calculated - I couldn't be more elated
to have realized today ...
all we talked about, all we walked about, all we fought about,
all we thought about - it's so much more then it seemed,
when you understand that you've made it to stand in the
reality of that universal high school teenage dream.

Parliaments - Katherine Grudens

I spend most nights
smoking parliaments in my parents' hot tub,
watching the smoke blend with the steam.
Losing sight of which is which,
of who I am,
of what I need.

The media tells me,
thin bones,
thick skin,
long fingernails,
short text messages,
short skirts,
tall stilettos.

But my body tells me something different.

My body tells me,
I am not
the media.

I need
warm milk,
skin on warm grass,
spoonful's of honey every morning.
Keeping myself soft
not weak.

Many people confuse the two.

My dad says I run in my dreams,
my blankets messy in the morning,
all my pillows on the floor,
redness smeared on my face like blood.

But what am I running from?

I always wake up wondering
if there are doctors out there,
that can cure this rotting inside of me.
The kind I can't explain.
The kind that rips my stomach open.
The kind that keeps my 22-year-old body
trapped.

In my parents' house.
In this steamy hot tub.
In the mouth of cigarette,
after cigarette.
Feeling more loved by them,
then anything else that has
touched my lips before.

And What of That Vortex - C.Streetlights

To freely enter that vortex
      sometimes called love
      (and sometimes Heaven, sometimes Hel)
is a celebration in vulnerability, no?

Yes.
A thrill in the terrifying risk
      of being loved just as vulnerably
      of ascending unto Heaven together
      of being thrust down to Hell
Passion burned once is worth passion burning forever, yes?

No.

To freely enter a vortex
      of once was and is no longer
        (thinking its love)
Is it forever caught spinning (whirling, dizzying)
      in its vortex
      evaporating up towards an eternal Heaven,

      or

      is there brittle disintegration before being sent
      to Hell?

(Did it exist at all?)

And what of the vulnerable,
do they remain in Heaven or Hell's vortex?

Yes.

Honesty - Natalie Caro

You've discovered forty-five ways to break your own heart.

1. Involves boys with absentee fathers.
2. Involves girls with mothers who couldn't love them.
3. Won't let you sleep at night.

4-40 You discovered all this with your therapist and can't talk about it without crying at the bar.

41. Makes you want to call her just to talk.

42. Reminds you that she was the closest you've come to friendship.

43. It isn't true, but you will pretend it is.

44. Feels like healing.

45. Was the closest you ever came to dying without carnations by your bed.

Perfect Girlfriend Learns the Word Normal
-Veronica Mattaboni

Perfect Girlfriend says yes, I *do* want to have sex with you in my
best friend's bed while she's in the shower.
Let's desecrate not only her personal space,
but also my respect for her.

Perfect Girlfriend says yes,
please fuck me in this camping tent that we are sharing with
four other sleeping people.
They won't mind.

Perfect Girlfriend says yes,
of course, I want to fool around on the couch after the movie we
were watching with my mother has ended
while she is still passed out on the adjacent couch.
Yes; of course.

Perfect Girlfriend says yes, because when Perfect Girlfriend says
no, Perfect Boyfriend says:

Don't you love me?
I do so much for you and you can't do this one thing for me?
If you love me then this shouldn't be a problem?
Maybe I'll go find someone who does care about me.
Other people do this all the time.
This is what Perfect Girlfriend is supposed to do.
And I don't understand what the big deal is anyway,
You're always getting crazy over nothing.
I don't see why this has to be a fucking fight every time.

Perfect Girlfriend says yes, I'm being irrational.
Yes, I'm being crazy.
See, Perfect Boyfriend can't wrap his head around the concept of
a panic disorder,
so Perfect Girlfriend gives it a name he can understand; says:
I just feel a little crazy today; I think my crazy is acting up;
That was totally crazy of me; I'm sorry I'm so crazy;

Perfect Girlfriend says yes, everything is fine.
Perfect Girlfriend is just seventeen,
thinks abuse can only look like black eyes,
too young to know she doesn't know any better.
Perfect Girlfriend has had much worse; this is the healthiest it's ever been;
she would do anything to keep her life this good.
So Perfect Girlfriend can't say no.

Sometimes, she tries to form the word *uncomfortable* and
Perfect Boyfriend says *Don't you think you're being a little crazy?*
and Perfect Girlfriend says yes.
But Perfect Boyfriend is only temporary, and the years go on
even though his presence in her life does not.
Older now, Perfect Girlfriend is with Normal Boyfriend.
And Normal Boyfriend doesn't know what to do.
He is afraid to touch her, because he knows Perfect Girlfriend can't say no.
He is afraid to ask because Perfect Girlfriend says yes, whether she wants to or not;
Hears *I don't see why this has to be a fucking fight every time* when the question is posed;
can imagine him walking out the door;
can't imagine doing the separation all over again.
Normal Boyfriend would rather not touch her at all than
accidentally make her do something she doesn't want to do.

Normal Boyfriend says *You can tell me no.*
Normal Boyfriend says *You don't have to do anything you don't want to.*
Normal Boyfriend says *Please don't try to be perfect for me. I don't want you to. Be whatever makes you feel comfortable: that's normal.*
Tell me no: that's normal.
Only do what you want to do: that's normal.

Perfect Girlfriend has never heard this before, does not know what to make of it; quickly learns there is no off switch on Perfect Girlfriend;
that perfect has been stitched into her impulse response.
She tries to pluck the threads from her anxiety like sutures, and learns that her muscle has grown around it, dissolving into their long-term memory.

Perfect Girlfriend still says yes,
still holds no in her throat like dipping land-locked toes in the ocean.
But she is trying,
wading in the water slowly,
adjusting to normalcy with stutters and setbacks and nervous laughter.

And this is the most herself she has ever felt.

Morning Glory - John Michael Antonio

After another fiery night
of cradling you and
watching you
fight your demons

I kiss you
in the first light of day
wanting to vanquish
your doubts and fears

In our fortress loft
above the roar of
the teeming
and luminous city

Love is alive
in spite of our
relentless enemies
and brutal miscalculations

You cling to me
angelic head on my chest
our legs entwined
skin to skin

I press you closer
you cling harder
sweet purple music
softly plays

First shadows
approach my teary eyes
and I am
speechless

And not worthy
to witness the
beauty I am
beholding

Hero – Natasha Alexander

The walls never scared you,
you knew breaking them down was never an option.
You didn't come with armor
or fancy words
Instead you came bare,
only you, and you climbed my wall brick by brick.
You moved so slowly,
I never even saw you coming

Once you were in,
you didn't try and fix me.
Instead you sat in silence
as you studied my pain
you came to understand my shame
and you loved me anyway.

I did need a Hero
but not one who came roaring in,
kicking up my dusty disgrace,
stepping on my broken pieces.
No I needed a Hero
who took his time,
one who treaded lightly.
I needed a Hero who would understand,
one who would stay regardless.
I needed a Hero who would love me gently.
I needed YOU.

Sunflowers and Sticky Tape - Jacqueline Cioffa

We built a house out of a dream
10 minutes turned into a life of sunflowers
and wooden porches
and Etta James
and Ella Fitzgerald
and thrift stores with old record players
and bread makers
and a light bulb on a string over the kitchen sink
and a couple in Sante Fe
and their gallery
and an old book of pictures of Texas from 1961 or was it 1959?
and a white Cadillac convertible with burgundy leather interior torn from age
and a steering wheel with sticky tape
and a motel with purple lights
and cactus in the desert
and a white bathing suit
and a black and white TV
and the same movie playing over and over
and Tequila with a worm
and the sunrise on the dunes in the desert
and the dark and the yellow line in the road
and the fork up ahead
and it's all in my mind
and my heart
and I did care
It was a lovely dream
I saw you today and paused short of breath
We had drifted away and apart

I wish you all your dreams of wooden houses
and dunes
and beaches
and bandanas
and cutoffs
and Hanes v neck t-shirts
and flip flops
and all
Take care and I do care
It was real for me
For a moment
and it was so nice to dream

A Man I Used to Love - Kelley Cooper

He was an avid reader. *New York Times* every morning, front to back.
He rode his bike to and from school, work, and the market.
He ate maple pecan granola each morning. He was a coffee snob.
He believed in spending $300 on a nice dinner without it having to be a special occasion. This is how he lived.
He appreciated art. He had a deep appreciation.
He loved good food, really good food. We ate well.
He joked a lot. He liked to tell me about raunchy phrases that made me cringe.
He smoked and then stopped.
He loved me. I loved him.
We stopped being kind. We started being mean.
I felt alone. I felt abandoned by my best friend.

Music. He was always in the know of the latest and greatest artists. He only went to concerts if he could sit in the front 3 rows. No exceptions.

When we went to NY for the first time, he explored the city while I slept. He feared nothing. He felt safe everywhere. This scared me and was also something I admired deeply.

We parted. We separated. Packed up the house. Split up the dishes and what not.
It ended. We ended.
He thinks of me. I think of him.
I was a hostess. He was a server.
He's a teacher. I am a life coach.
He taught me how my heart could break and heal.

Bad Things - Dori Owen

*"And all those shadows they're filled up with doubt.
I wanna do bad things with you." --Jace Everett, Bad Things*

Nirvana
was
lying
for days
sharing a
too small bed
we were
two commas
a perfect fit

It was all
so easy
so fine
so good
does my memory lie
and hide bad things?

So in love with you I was
I knew you loved me first
you made
me laugh
oh, God
how I love silly
your notes
made up words
New Yorker cartoons
Music man
you knew where
you were going
while
purpose eluded me
I chose wine and weed
instead

does my memory lie
and hide bad things?
I see photos
young
we were so young
two kids
playing house in
tiny spaces
we called home
in 90210
Then
you took Europe
I took LA
a continent divide
just like us
I did wonder
I did think
would he
could he
but it was
much too far
much too late
and marriage
eventually
sent me an
invite

In time
you found your fame
I found my career
haven't seen you
in a lifetime
an unexpected
contact
has jarred my thoughts
to things long ago
locked away

does my memory lie
and hide bad things?

I am not foolish
I know I was
the one
who made mistakes
hurt you
ran over you
again
and
again
and again once more

I writhe with guilt
thinking
thinking
thinking
how could I be
so unkind
to someone
so kind
does my memory lie
and hide bad things?
Undecided
if I want
forgiveness from
you
or
forgiveness from
me
How would life be
if I'd gone with you
should I have
could I have
never will I know
does my memory lie
and hide bad things?

Now I'm grown
and know how
to behave
with a man
like you
my apologies they ring
so shallow

It's an eternity
too late
and you are far, far away
but, yes
my memory did lie
I now know
I did do bad things

And somewhere
in the
continent divide
is someone
who loved you
I really did

Romantics - Richard DeFino

I know how you resent smoking, but what if
I was to tell to you that my love for you was
eternal, and as I said this, I took a long drag from my favorite
menthol flavored cigarette, would you still resent smoking?

Or what if I, on double bended knee, admitted to you just
how pointless my life would be if you were to leave me.
What if I told you this after I took an obnoxious sized sip of
my favorite Bourbon.
I know how much you hate me to drink.

What if that happened?
What if I could only be truthful while hurting you?
Would I be a selfish lover, or a thoughtful fool?

Or could it just be that I require my feelings to be masked
and
riddled with chemicals in order to coax my fear of loving
another human?
Upon the validity of my words tonight,
I will hurt this time,
but this time,
I am clean.

For reasons unknown to myself,
I cannot put the words together in a sentence,
to tell you
just how I feel.

I recoil at the sight of us,
locking eyes,
but this comes with the highest and sincerest form of flattery.
I fear spewing incorrect logic of how I perceive our love,
what my idea of romance is.

I am the homeless man on the street that pedestrians and
tourist avoid making eye contact with.
I come flawed.
You appear perfect to me.
But you are flawed as well.
Your only mistake was choosing to love me.

Apparitions - Susan P. Blevins

Online dating's long parade of hopefuls, liars, and scammers fills a seemingly endless pipeline that like a sewer, spews into my inbox.

There was Bill, retired plastic surgeon, pleasant enough but looked like a corpse.
Turned out he was a cancer survivor. No problem, but his negative attitude was.

Beau was the chicken-necked attorney with a passion for making pizza and for his dachshunds who sleep in his bed. All fine except for the twitching of his scrawny neck in an overlarge collar.

Now Peter was something else - he worked for a communications company and when
we talked politics he said he thought that Hitler was an idealist. Another goner...

Then there was Frank, so short that even in flatties I towered above him. But that was nothing compared to his bad body odor, bad breath and stinky car. And he grabbed me for a kiss! Next...

Later came Dan the pilot. Italian extract, stocky and into sex. Good chemistry, but oh dear, survivor of prostate cancer, which made sex a slog. And oops, I forgot. He was married.

Along came Norman, who ranted on about his life with never a question about me. After four
and a half narcissistic hours we ended our rendezvous with a prayer. Deliver me Oh Lord.

But Juan! After cocktails and dinner and lively conversation, he accompanied me to my car and proceeded to kiss me like there was no tomorrow. Pity. Turned out there *was* no tomorrow.

The one who takes the cake though is Bert, the attorney who earns his living not in law
but cultivating pot in his guest bathroom. A 400 pound 65-year old pothead. What a waste.

Next came Robert, whose wife died next to him while walking down a dark street, both oblivious to the car (or so he says) that mowed her down, and one month later, so lonely he's dating online.

I really fancied Lenny from Chicago though. Good chemistry and great kissing, but he was one of the disappearers who turn up sporadically then vanish. My guess is he's married.

Lou was the experiment, my first black guy, attractive, fit, obviously into sex but
let me tell you, when push comes to shove, a 60-year old dick is a 60-year old dick.

I was almost forgetting TJ, pleasant and charming, married and divorced five times,
but his forte, so he assured me, was working as part of a marital team. Really?

Endless procession going nowhere. If nothing else, they provide entertainment for
my girlfriends in exercise class. "We live vicariously through you," they tell me.

There are many more, but I'll stop here. They can go in another poem of remembrance.
Dating in older age takes stamina, commitment, and a healthy sense of humor.

Turn the Page - Margret Avery

Where do you go when your heart is aching
Where do you speak to free
yourself of loving
the one who didn't
stand beside you
loving the one who didn't
find you
in the moments that mattered the most
in the moments like he was a ghost
not there
but there
physical
staring
empty and judgmental.
So turn the page
in your life
and start to look and skip
to another person's day
to another person's way.
You now may not want
another pattern
that feels like your
moon is conjunct with Saturn
and play to the rhythm of
what the unknown leads
but go to the place where peace
and love will proceed.

Promises in the Dark - John Michael Antonio

As OMD still sings
about hopes and dreams
and the ephemeral
light of summer fades
I know my love
for you never will

Oh baby
those nights
we disappeared
laughing and speeding
into the night
in my freedom fighting Camaro

The vibrancy of the moment
telling us that we were
born to be alive

Reaching that sacred summit
champagne city below
toasting the
irresistible future
with the fresh
starlight in your eyes

You took my heart
and gave me yours

And I made you
soft and enduring
promises in the dark

I am yours
I am yours
I am yours

Then, Now and Forever

My Addiction - F.K. Jadoon

You are my addiction,
so sweet and tempting,
like the aroma of my favorite meal,
that I cannot resist, or taste.

My path to self-destruction.
Like an alcoholic doomed to die,
yet, he continues on drinking,
knowing that it's death in itself.

My very personal alluring hell,
that I cannot stop, but to burn in.
Knowing that I'll be devastated.
Knowing that it's hell,
however pleasant.

My sweetest nightmare,
that I dread,
yet marvel at.
That I cannot stop hoping to see,
Day after day…

With an increasing passion, that burns me.
Inside and out…

My own drug that kills me.
Oh! So sweetly,
silently,
devastatingly.

But intoxicates me into oblivion,
nonetheless,
relieving me of the pain,
though temporarily.
Ensuring that I do not part with it.

I Am Your Addict.
And you are,
My addiction.

F1 Generation - Tennessee Hill

He was dripping amber, the color of burst fuses.
I cut myself on his lips, jagged stone jaw.
I was pistachio green, growing under
stucco stones with worms and snow.
We crossed over, a piece to the other like
a schoolyard trade. At the end of us, the spiral years,
we were a mess of gray, which was not our in between color.
There was too much of him or too little me or maybe
when people crash into each other, expecting to bleed
the blood of one another, it is the Hollywood notion
that love is pink and red and there.

Someday Someway - Dori Owen

If someone should ask
what is a regret?
I would answer
truthfully and say
not mastering
how to stay.

I've pretended to sleep
with men who loved me
and some
I have loved back.
I do find myself
in spite of myself
plotting
escape routes
instead of
savoring sweet dreams.

A man
once dubbed me
uncontainable.
I thought it was banter
and laughed.
Instead it became
an anthem
a self-fulfilling prophecy.

It may be a defense
a fear of being left first
or perhaps
I'm a chimera
in disguise.

But please
don't misunderstand
I have not canceled
chasing my happily ever after.
Instead of passages out
I'll soon be planning ways to stay.

*"If you can't tell me what you need
All I can do is wonder why
Someday, someway
Maybe I'll understand you"
--Marshall Crenshaw*

House Keys - Elizabeth Regen

That first day I didn't like your voice and I wanted you replaced.
I didn't like your jacket and I didn't want you in the space.
You left before the rest- like you were the best ...
And I scoffed and I rolled my eyes.
I could have picked any other guy.
You showed up again- and the day after that too-
And then suddenly I was becoming familiar to you – and you to me ...
I was waiting to see
If there was more to it or was it just in my head- me laying next to you in bed ...
But the heat seeping out of my pores when my body was touching yours made me want to taste your mouth and I did.
And I hid that I wanted more of you in me-
See- the situation was infatuation and I couldn't get you out of my head-
I think I was on your mind too- because others were telling me – there's more to this- "him & you."
He's watching you when you don't know.
He's following you everywhere you go.
I didn't notice ... I didn't see ...
There were things inside you that were parts of me.
I'd lost them I thought-
Somewhere in the nineties.
I thought I'd found them once
In a set of house keys ...
But no.
I spoke. You laughed.
I smiled. You asked ...
Things that I hadn't heard in a long time. Things I gave away ... Things that used to be mine.
I love you. And I miss you deep in my heart.
I do. I did. Really. Right from the start.

No Wonder - Natasha Alexander

No wonder you came looking for someone like me.
No wonder my strangeness never scared you off,
instead you laughed at me and enfolded me in your embrace.

No wonder you have found peace in the chaos of our relationship,
No wonder the madness gave you a bizarre sense security.

I've often wondered how you ended up choosing me
The wild at heart...
...a complicated mess

We're crazy at times. But I get it now.

Each scream is filled will an undeniable realness, each fit with authenticity.

We don't form some facade of how you are supposed to love, or what is expected of you to be accepted...if we don't feel it in our deepest being.
No, we don't march like soldiers.
Rather, we dance to the rhythm of our hearts and to the beat of our pulse.

They silence their anger, because that's not what "good people" do or say or act.
This was the way you were taught...the life you had to suppress.

No, no, no!!!
When we get mad, we SCREAM from the top of our lungs.
When we get sad, we CRY and we WEEP like mad men.
When we are confused, we ASK questions and debate until our minds and souls are satisfied.
And when we love, we LOVE with everything we are made of.

We dance this dance together; we dance to our own music.
They don't understand and shake their heads while gossiping behind their hands.
But in truth they are missing out.
Because we're the ones on the dancefloor and they're the ones watching.

I get it now...
You choose us because in this roller-coaster,
no matter how scary it gets, you can be just "YOU"
You don't have to be silenced or misunderstood.
You don't have to explain why and how.

I get it now...
With me, you are finally free.

The Revealing - John Michael Antonio

along the road of differences
precious stones of similarities
are deliciously found
so please take your time
you are worth the wait
slowly and surely
for the rest of our lives
reveal yourself to me
as I reveal myself to you
I want to see everything
hear everything
feel everything
about you
I want to shoulder your dreams
and push them forward
earn your trust and never have you regret it
catch your tears on my shirt
and smooth away your heartbreaks
make your enemies
my enemies
help you fight off
the wolves of everyday life
and watch you
win baby win

How to Love a Wanderer - Nicole Lyons

If you happen to stumble upon a wanderer,
unlock the door
and welcome them in; but do so knowing
that they're only there to rest their feet.
Don't offer to unpack their bags, instead
fill them to brimming and leave them
beside the back door, uncluttered and easy
to reach. Stoke the fire, put the kettle on,
and guard your heart.
It's passion and pain that nurture the unsettled.
Embrace them for the moment, delight in their tales,
and commit them
to memory... when the sun rises
they'll be gone,
pack full of hearts, soul bursting
with restlessness, leaving you
incredibly richer, and devastatingly poorer,
all at the same time.

Phantom Heart – Julie Anderson

Lover your name is true.
I see you beyond what has been ingrained
honeyed words drip from your lips, drop into my dreams.
Beat on for me, I can hear you in my heart.

Sigh deeply suck me in.
Spin a web of wishes around the sincere fantasy.
Exhale the spite of temperance.
Patiently waiting.

Chimera of reality fading quickly despite intrinsic detail.
Phantom heart, yours is mine.
We are like the others caught off guard
thinking why did you call out for me across time?

You ask me to believe what is not appropriate.
Specter of sin
I will follow
resigned to seek the fountain of your love.

In a trance
I hear the beat.
Phantom Lover
when will the inception begin?

Is it fate?
You are forbearer of doom.
Liar, love is a mirage.
Fool that I am I believed your whispers.
My lips cannot taste your love.
Delusion is the gift you offer.
Phantom Heart
let me go

Devotion to lust, sticky sickly sweet
is not true?
Enchanted we are, not for others
in dreams, our desire remains.

Phantom lover kiss me once
like honest people do.
Slide me in your heart, take me
make evident your intention.

Charlatan of emotion, desperately seeking a home
you cannot animate what is denied.
Phantom Lover murmur once more
I can feel you in my heart.

You Are Mine — SA Smith

I love the way you see the world.
Full of life, full of love.
You show me things I never knew.
You bring color to my world by just being you.

I was so lonely.
Sure, I put on a good show.
Let people think, let people know.
That I was strong, that I needed no one.
But you knew, you saw right through my heart,
Straight into my soul.

You reached into my cold world and gave me your hand.
You pulled me in and never let me go.
You cherished me, kept me close.
You protected me.

I am so lucky you chose me.
You could have had anyone.
Someone with less baggage.
Someone with less curves.
Someone with more money.

But you chose me,
out of everyone in the world,
you chose me.

I am grateful for that every day.
Thanking the universe for this amazing man.
For the partner I get to laugh with in the morning.
For the strong arms that wrap around me at night.
For the body and the mind, I am so enamored.

Thank you for breaking down my walls,
and showing me love.

Thank you for making me feel special
every moment of our life.

Thank you for building a world with me,
I am proud to be a part of.

Most of all, thank you for loving me through it all.
The ups, the downs, the highs and the lows.
You are my rock, my light in the storm.
You are my best friend and my greatest love.

I am so thankful to call you mine.

Love Notes From Humanity

LOSS

Love Notes From Humanity

The Ocean is a Woman - Megan Garner

The ocean is a woman.
She is vast and she is changing,
And she does not hide from us
All her forms, all her shades,
All her faces.

But we see her stilled, at times,
And we assume passiveness.
We see calm waters
And, in forgetting her power,
We abuse our own.

We fill her with waste,
Hateful, little things
Unnatural bits and melting scraps
That add and add upon each other
And make a weight in the pit of her.

And though she feels this,
She cannot speak.
She cannot speak
Because she has lost her voice.
We assume she never had one.
We have chosen to forget her sound.
Her waves, her depth, and
Her ability to recount—to remember:

Every anchor dropped,
Scraping in her, digging.
Every spill left running,
Staining her and spreading.
We do not listen
To the moans of the ships.
For they do know,
Even though she is silent.

They feel it as they cut through her
They find the truth of her pain.

In that moment,
When she is opening under them,
She reveals her Spirit.
She reveals her Self.
But these are only caught in passing.

And we see, too,
Far removed on the shore.
We admire her beauty and sadness alike
We gaze, slack-jawed, at her magnitude,
Her magnificence,
Loving her, yet fearing her.

When she reaches for us, we run away
She pushes forward, and we pull back,
Because we remember what we've done.
And we are ashamed.

We tell ourselves things.
She is in God's place, this deep dwelling
Where she may slosh and rumble
And peak all she wants.
Why should she want for more
When she has settled so nicely,
And for so long, in this place?
In this pit of sand, just for her.

Isn't just one place enough
For a voiceless thing?

Sapling - Tiffani Burnett Velez

You never came even though you had a promise date. I imagined your face a tiny smooth circle of pinkish flesh. You slipped from us, disappeared in ash, when they tossed you on the dewy grass where the roses grow. I left you there for 11 years.

But the guilt of you made me restless to open wide the windows and to make new memories out of what could have been. But you flew out on the waves of your siblings' laughter and on their quickening heights and goals and wrestling. Now I no longer see you, even in my dreams.

Still, you have not left us, not really. You're a tree that grows in the shadow of our movements, a sapling in a high forest that we hike. You're still silent and faceless, but we let the rain grow your roots. The mourning dove rests in other branches now, and when I see her there, I know that you were made for this.

Bare Bones of It - Tabitha Stirling

'Don't throw me to the wolves', I said
but cancer had your brain by then. Along
with bone, and skin and hair.
I have things to tell you that I couldn't.
I am a late starter, lost my virginity at 18
to the video repair man, in the spare
bedroom with the rough navy blue sheets
you bought from Peter Jones.

My children love you best even though
you have a radiance that they can't see.
When I was ill you would give me
asparagus soup from the can. And
Lucozade with its flashy orange cellophane
coat. Not out of place on a Kings Cross
night. And I would drink it carefully
sipping your love, like fine wine.

I used to crack jokes about you to
make my father like me better. They
were cheap shots, Babycham insults.
Mocking your terror of tunnels and
lifts, dark, sharp places that chopped
you off at your knees. Then I
remember you dancing on 7 Mile Beach,
the inky night a Covent Garden backdrop.
A fourth daiquiri in your hand,
you were a Goddess.

And people sent you crazy ideas about
cures. Rattlesnake venom, aloe vera and
blessings from some Saint who didn't give a
fuck. I cursed God in the night, rocking
your Grandson, salted fury coursing
and how I hated. Everything.
Wait for me in those fields of gold,
I'll come when it's time. But for now,
tracing the outline of a photograph
slamming the drawer shut, quick before
tears come, because that is all for now.

First Hours of Forever - Elizabeth Regen

It's the kind of deep sorrow
....That leaves just BLACK
Where there should be tomorrow

And it's the kind of harrowing pain
....That leaves a burning HOLE
Where there should be a stain...

It's not just cold at night
...It's FREEZING
And when it starts to get dark
I wonder if I'm still breathing...
All of these long
first hours of forever
Never
stop coming.
These strangling waves of time
are more than unkind.
They're pure torture.
I thought "You're alive!"
But then I woke up -
and it wasn't even a dream
it was just a thought I had
in between
asleep and awake...
A very tiny break from
the never-ending-ness of it-
the foreverness of it...
the absolute certainty of it.
Dead. Is this what it means?
It seems to be a team of minutes that bully the center of my soul...
Taunting and haunting the halls of my memory...
Forcing me to ask myself over & over
"How can this be?"
"How can this be?"
"Where are you?"
"PLEASE ANSWER ME!"

It's the kind of insanity
...that leaves no TRACKS

It's the sort of MADNESS
that expects him to come back.

Pick up the phone....

Please don't leave me here alone.

Walk through the door...
 Like you always have before...
 Like you always have before...

Before.

You Rise - Kim Sisto Robinson

(For my dear sister, Kay, I'm so sorry I couldn't save you.)

Your face is fading.
I see shadows of chin,
cheekbone,
childhood inside my mind.

Orange Kool-Aid,
baloney sandwiches,
Aunt Carol's peonies like colossal,
pink faces thrill us.

He loves me, he loves me not.

You tell me you lost your virginity
in the backseat of an 85 Chevy.
I tell you Sylvia Plath's poetry saved
me from sticking my head inside an oven.

I am, I am, I am.

Our ovaries jump up and down like
two schoolgirls exposing secrets.
Nobody ever got me like you,
loved me like you.

In my dreams,
he doesn't murder you.
We are laughing,
smearing charcoal- Madonna eyeliner
on one another,
Bonne Bell vanilla gloss.

I am terrified of loss,
unfinished sentences,
letting go.
I only know a world with you
inside my air.

Your hair covers me like a dark water,
long strands caught between my teeth,
fractured prayers beneath,
distant,
a silent god.

A thick, rolling fog.

In my dreams,
you are unreachable,
untouchable,
sitting on a ledge,
an edge,
leaning away.

From me.

When I awaken,
your name is
written upon my lips,
your voice lifts
like a million brilliant birds.

You slide next to me in words.

Your veins pump with history,
halleluiahs,
home.
Your story climbs
from stone,
from the grave,
the soil—

You rise. You rise. You rise.

My Lover Does Not Deserve Black
—Elizabeth Kirkpatrick Vrenios

I wear scarlet to his funeral,
a beautiful floor-length affair
with sleeves
that flick the air like flames,
a splash of red electricity.

I swirl with the bagpipe's skirls.
Sounds hunchbacked and keening,
drench the mourners
crushed in black,
mute and dark eyed.

I am the solitary scarlet bell.

My throat torn open,
pours out scarlet grief
splashes the sky,
stains my skin,
and smears the air with roses.

Presence in Absence - Paakhi Bhatnagar

You are an omnipresent cold embrace,
that keeps me shivering
through the empty nights.

You are the dawn of day
and the moon, that blinds me
and keeps me awake.

You are a ceaseless string of memories
in my lucid dreams; and
the jolt of somnambulism.

You are a sinking ship,
that drowns me slowly,
whenever I close my eyes.

You leave me wandering
flitting on sidewalks,
seeing through clouded eyes.

You are a facade of beauty
but a whirl of sleepless nights; and
drowsy days.

You are an insomniac piece of me.
And I feel you when the sky is crippling,
into fragments of oblivion.

I feel you when
the ghostly darkness
has engulfed my bones and pinched my skin.

I feel you when
I cannot feel anything.
And I understand that there is presence in absence.

The Colour of Us – Nicole Lyons

Water is wet and grass is green and

we are us… until it isn't… and we aren't…
anymore.

And that's how it was, he and I, right
from the start: peas and carrots,
sand and surf, heaven and hell.

We were the late night phone calls that went straight
to voicemail, the last light in the window
when all other doors were locked.

We were voracious laughter muffling horrified screams.
We were bodies twisted in ecstasy and minds broken in
angst. We were psych stays and breakdowns, pills popped
and death threats, sirens wailing and holding cells.

We were life, on a September morning, and death on
an April night. And in our own minds we were golden.

Transformation - F.K. Jadoon

And then the day came...
That dark, dreadful day that we'd feared for so long...
And when it did
Everything changed,
Everything came to an end...
But it was already 'written'
That it had to end, that it will end
Because it was never 'destined to happen' after all!

You became just a name in so many names...
A bitter-sweet memory, in so many memories...
But unlike all the names, all the memories...
You left a mark on my soul
somewhere very deep inside me...
Every word, every feeling
You etched it on the horizon of my being...
And I transformed...
just like an ugly caterpillar transforms into a beautiful butterfly.

There was nothing left of my old self anymore
Because "I" was not the same as before!
You had torn me open and then sewed me back together again
Into such 'unknown' intricate patterns,
And my parts were stitched so differently now
That I could not fathom the 'transformation' that took place inside me...
You were the 'transformer' of my being
The catalyst that brought me to my own 'end'...

The Skin I'm In, Loved and Lost - Brianna Scott

I.

Everyday I try
I try to move on, I try to forget, I really do
But it seems as though it is impossible for me
My heart won't allow me to forget the way he made me feel
Me, an enticing vixen creature as I stared into his eyes
I gave him the power to control the very raw,
uncut human functions
Society likes to keep packed away tightly
in a little box
in the corner.
Me,
with a slight movement,
up and down- side to side,
I could break his carefully fixed facade
for a moment.
He gave me that power to feel
I can not forget/ escape the feeling
Everyday I try
I try to move on, I try to forget, I really do
My body is physically mourning the loss
for too long now,
It has been empty
Only a certain length,
girth can fit in it
Until then it will punish me
Stabbing my uterus from the inside
Shedding its walls in the most painless way possible
Never letting me forget
the pleasure it once felt.

II.

I love that we can't have casual conversation
I love being treated like your whore
I love that you don't even bother to keep the appearances up
I love being treated like a cum dumpster
A receptacle
A fish you forget to feed

An intangible object
An objectifiable woman
Open for business
I love crying crying crying
I love that I've put so more effort into this than I thought
I love the depreciating value of my pussy
I love that I was so dumb to believe a horny 18 year old boy
I'd love to die
Of embarrassment
second hand embarrassment
Depression
A panic attack
Cardiac arrest
Fuck you

III.

I waited
In the car
I waited in the rain
The dark
Shaved it all
Just to be pretty
And thom York blaring
The gutairs melting
I waited
For the rain to stop
For you to say sorry
My feather brain
Your masculinity
The airplane doors to open
To climb in
And I'm waiting
For a text
A call
A sign from God
Waiting
For a sink hole to give me hope
To swell me up
Then suck me in
And suck me dry
And I'm waiting-

Beautiful Cage - Natasha Alexander

Charming as a Prince
I'm envied by all as he leads me into my cage
One covered in flowers
draped in diamonds
A place where he lays his world at my feet.

I never want for anything, as he showers me with riches.
Yet his tone is deaf to what my heart longs
The song my soul screams, goes unnoticed
My cries lost in the wind,
He fears me leaving
Then orders for a cashmere blanket to wrap me up in
But so tight, it chafes my skin.
I sit in my beautiful cage and stare
at the freedom I ache for.

He notices distress on my face but
I smile on cue
as he cuffs me
with yet another string of pearls.

Sensing my need to escape,
He paces up and down while he glares
at my every stir
I stop moving

He strides closer
to count my breaths
I stop breathing

So I die in silence waiting to exhale
...in my beautiful cage.

Elements on Fire - Rachel Thompson

It's all in the ending, regardless of how it begins, causing water to steam, fire to crackle, earth to heat, air to move. The elements are angry, my worry stones tell me, as I roll them across my aching fingers, as they jump, biting at my bones.

Heavy bones, tired of the weight I carry, this burden of a love I'm supposed to feel, one that is written and raised, sun pinging off a peeling, faded golden seal, all perfunctorily created in some airy office in California by an hourly clerk I've never met. Intimacy marked by agency, diametrically opposed.

What a strange little dance we've created, this business of love, that which started from binding twine or ribbon to one-upmanship in millions of dollars in flowers that die, of clear, shiny rocks pulled out of caves on the backs of babies, of twinkly lights that carry no meaning. Yet, if every intimacy of marriage is different, how is it that the human condition of energy and fluid exchange is no different? The song remains the same.

My body moves me forward because that's where I'm supposed to be. I can't go back to that silent place of quiet fury and prickly doubt, feeling my worry stones compelling me to go, move, jump, girl!

Taking responsibility, blaming myself, for not creating enough crackling fire or earthy warmth, yet in the end it wasn't about that, really.

It's not about me, or him, or us. It's not about shedding the skins of blame, or dusting the detritus of what little clarity remains. It's about the energy surrounding us, undulating in circular waves and unseen, infinite patterns.

It's a lie that all the elements work together in unison -- they fight for prominence, just as we fight for the one we need, filling our core, giving us life.

I needed air to move.

To end.

To begin.

Broken – SA Smith

Broken, less than ... that's how I feel.
A shadow of the person I am supposed to be.
Never able to finish what I plan or hope to accomplish.
Always checking to see how I feel. Have I overdone? Will the pain be too much?
I feel like a pain. A pain to the people that depend on me most.

I am supposed to be strong.
I am supposed to be brave.
I am supposed to be able to stand up and be the me I have always been.
Be a mom, be a wife, be a woman that is independent and enchanted with life.

I am less than.

I take it hour by hour, day by day.
Hoping that I can do it, hoping I can get through it.
Making excuses to call away the pain.
Hoping that maybe they don't see it in my eyes – the pain, the sadness, the feeling of despair.
Hoping that maybe they won't see what is really going on.
Hoping that maybe today I won't have to breakdown and decide what has to be done, and what I can put off for yet another day.

Hope is what I still have ... that the pain hasn't yet taken away.
Every day is another day, every day a different degree of me.
Mostly broken, mostly less than ... but still hopeful that tomorrow will be better.

Humanity - Hasty Words

Once again
I am her
The accused
Standing
Awaiting
Retribution
For crimes
For words
For pain
Caused
Not innocent
I plead guilty
On all counts
The mask
I wear is a gift
From me to you
Saving you
From having
To lay eyes on
The hideous
Creature
Hiding beneath

Damaged Goods - Dave Pacailler

I am damaged goods.
I am forever broken.
I am beyond repair.
That is my excuse.

I have not known innocence.
My parents were self-absorbed.
They were strangers,
they ignored me.
I grew up alone, a defiant adolescent.
Rejection, neglect and disdain were normal.
I sought comfort from
strangers,
substances,
selfish desires.
I learned to disguise my pain with laughter.
I learned my self-respect was shattered.

I have not known distress.
My silence melts it away.
I have success,
portraying strength.
Yet I am weak, a fragile creature.

Reckless, callous, and hardened I've become.
I seek comfort from
my affliction,
my anger,
my aching.
I learned to hurt the people who love me.
I learned to embrace the ghosts that haunts me.

I have not known affection.
My camouflage hides my shame.
Yet I have friends,
they're my addictions.
They understand me, they sympathize.
Shelters, harbors, and temples they've become.

I seek comfort from
cravings,
compulsions,
coercions.
I learned to keep my walls well-guarded.
I learned to accept this fate disheartened.

That is my excuse.
I am beyond repair.
I am forever broken.
I am damaged goods.

Unhappy Girl – Stephanie Ortez

The hot, humid morning of July woke her up.
The cool sheets couldn't contain the fire inside her body
A familiar sensation she'd thought had vanished regained
momentum in the monotony of her life.
"I can't get up, I can't face it"
She was the product of an unsatisfactory life.
Almost wishing the sun could burn the anxieties accumulated
within herself,
blinding her vision to reconcile being at ease.
Her sudden frailty,
withholding the weight of her struggles,
she felt voiceless,
she no longer wanted an identity.
She couldn't devote herself to the philosophy carried by
others,
feeling comfortable and complacent of their daily tasks.
The humid sensation has vanished,
the icy perception of realism invades her once again.
Could she ever resemble that faithful image of feeling pure,
the richness of a life with dreams?
It didn't matter how enthusiastic she seemed while the sun
gazed upon her face,
her fate was sealed at night,
alone.
Hearing the clock ticking
knowing the electric sensation of what is real,
past,
or future
is lost in cold reasoning.
The hot,
humid night of July caught her.
Lost in a valley of words that echo in her tormented soul,
composed of ecstasy and agony.

UnLoveAble – Julie Anderson

Don't hold my hand.
Never hug me, kiss me
or tell me that you love me.

Always say things that stab my heart.
That is the way it should be.
What you feel is more important than my thoughts,
so please continue to speak over me.

Every mistake I have made,
color them in with a bold marker
Tell me about all the times that I have failed in love
failed my family.
Remind me,
because sometimes I prefer to forget.

Keep me hanging,
keep me on a leash.
keep me confused
keep me desperate
keep me

My decisions are the wrong ones
that is why you always reprimand me.
True love.
Yes it is true love.
The way you take loving control over me.

It doesn't matter that you will not sleep with me
I know that you can't stand me.
I won't beg.
I don't need to feel your body next to mine

I am arrogant
A narcissist,
the kind of woman you abhor.

Efforts that I make to better myself are never quite right.
I am happy that you call me out on that fact.
I have to try harder.
Be better.

I am foolish.
I am a child
locked in a fucked up woman's body.

I am unlovable.

I Promise - Icess Fernandez

How do I tell you that you are beautiful?

How do I tell you that it's not your fault?
That when I left your house I was plenty strong enough.
That you are a good mother,
that the world hasn't been as cruel to me as you think.

How do I make you understand that I am sick beyond chicken soup?
That when I cannot breathe it is not because you are smothering me.
That when I cry it is not because we are poor.

You watch me in a state we call sleep but it isn't,
that's where demons are fought.
You pray over me to make sure I wake up the next morning.
You wrestle with the echoes of past lives
Of the little girl you carried
Of the little girl you taught to read
Of the little girl standing tall.

You think to yourself, "I have failed her."
The woman who returned was not
the one who left.

Your silent anger,
In the looks toward the North
when things are mentioned
your jaw clenches.
Your fingers stuff themselves into fists
under tables, behind backs.

"Esa vieja mal nacida," you start.
You stop.
You change the subject.

You cannot fight off the bullies any more than
I can fight the urge to kill myself.
These are the bullies you cannot see.
The ones you cannot punch.
The ones you cannot chingar la madre.

These are the bullies you hoped wouldn't come for me.
Yet, they are here, in your house, on the couch, sipping cafe con leche.

But that doesn't stop you from lighting a candle

Making me soup. Watching me sleep.
Mama, you are beautiful. It is not your fault. I am sick.
But I promise, tonight, I won't kill myself if you hold my hand while I sleep.

Bi-Polar Love - Tabitha Sterling

We had a chaotic reverie.
We united as a weary
autumn storm pissing on
rusty love.

The times you filmed me
drooling my savior complex.
The times you watched me
peeling gum off the night sky.

You indulged your mania and
stuckmagnetsonthefridgeand
pluckedicyoystermeatand
tooklibertieswithbaths.

You howled about your illness
I had dignity in mine.
I grabbed the world by its ass
You puked it up overnight.

Evanescence - Nicole Lyons

I swear I was clean before you came blazing in,
guns firing hot, bursting into me
with pain so sweet
that I begged for a slow death.
But you stole the sweet
ache from my bones
and left the savage bits of you behind,
spraying them all over my world.
They blot out the sun,
and leave me with a forever night.
They crawl over me, inside of me,
and consume me with the filth of memories.
And they whisper
about this slow death
and how I should be careful
what I wish for.

V.5 - Rachel Convery

give me the gun, my love
this is no dance, no
punchline

blue smoke coiling like hollow wire
above the spruce crowns, glittered

with the last cold
of the cruelest month

the tired ladder
propped beside the gutter
clotted scarlet

the knifesong of the wind
beyond the grasp
of the fire

a slap, a fist to the throat
or to the bones

the safety's off, you turned
all your loaded words
on yourself

My Heart Tastes Like Chicken - Lela Casey

I gave you my heart,
ripped it from my chest
where it lay comfortably nestled
between lily white rib bones
and family dinners in front of the television.

You picked it up daintily
between your fingers
as if it weren't alive,
as if it weren't throbbing madly,
as if it weren't spilling blood all down your white shirt.

You took one nibble,
then another.
Some pieces you rolled around on your tongue,
let slide slickly down the back of your throat.
Others you sucked clean,
until the raging scarlet of my insides turned to a pale pink on your lips.

One bite was distasteful to you,
so you spit it out.
I watched as it dribbled from your mouth
and tumbled to the floor
where the cat gobbled it to bits

You rose up from your chair and turned away from me,
chunks of my heart trailed behind you
like bread crumbs for the vultures.
Stop! I whispered.

If you don't want it, give it back to me!
It's all I have
You turned back and smiled at me,
sinewy bits stuck between your teeth.
"It tastes like chicken"

What It Was Worth- Catherine Zickgraff

For a while I follow your blue eyes glowing off the stereo,
then tuck myself into you, inhaling your smell, remembering
our summer in my four-poster bed. You wrapped me in
your robe, we passed joints in the sunlight of my bathtub.

At night, you laid your muscle under my pillow. And in
the blue light of the TV, I nestled my back in your chest.

But it's drizzling tonight in the headlights, they glide by the
main road that passes the lake. In the back seat, you hold
me under your arm—your pants unzipped, me breathless.

I reach my cigarette out your window, but the orange pit falls
inside the car, shattering like fireworks onto my panties.

That disappearing lace is how jealousy burns when you
tell me later a new chick was in your head even then.

Playing For Keepsies – C. Streetlights

I think,
(perhaps)
it was when you
played my heart
as yet another marble in a circle.

Lining your shooter,
you knuckled down –
carelessly –
finding Me
inside the chalk dust.

I was just another glass duck,
(nothing important to add to your collection)

No matter.

You were playing for keepsies.
Everyone else plays for points.

Before I knew it:
I was shot out of the ring
just another casualty of fudging
(while nobody was looking)
Pocketed and then forgotten,
tossed aside and then dumped.

I thought.
And waited.

Seasons change.

(again)

Little boys pull out their chalk
to draw their circles.
They rummage around dusty old drawers,
to find forgotten marbles
that once shined and reflected light.

They try to polish the glass,
scratched and dull from past abuse.

(Good enough, they think.)

Here we are again, you and I –
You toss me in the dirt;
your shooter is once again ready to take aim.

Only this time is different.
This time you aren't prepared
for the sun in your eyes.

And it's bright.

While You Were Away – Julie Anderson

While you were away
I walked through shadows disguised as glass
I danced alone
I learned that I could
feel,
be just as I am

While you were away
freedom delivered me to heaven.
I found my voice
spoke for myself,
enjoyed the words
said them again and again

While you were away
a taste for whisky developed on my tongue
I devoured raw flesh,
felt another
kind of emotion
swaying on my feet,
balancing on hope
I can see there is a way

While you were away
laughter reigned,
my heart expanded
anxiety lifted, floated away
I discovered my strength

While you were away,
I finally became me.

First Try - Elizabeth Regen

Vague, repetitious, harrowing flashbacks -
And wondering if it'll ever happen again.
Why not?
If it did before and then again,
Even in the mean times and always in the ever after?
Realizing and Rationalizing -
Roller coasters on a roof top during an
External Blizzard
Internal Blizzard
And a flickering cigarette burned straight through that '78-hour midnight run
To melt them both away...

Perfect, deadly, homemade concoction of paranoia -
Self-hate, despair and so much lost once again.
Defeat sets in
like decay and with no excuses or reasons,
No differentiation between the seasons or those who will
Cry
Tonight because of you.
Like a cavity, you try to fill it,
Drill through it,
the rotten darkness and clean it out.
So it won't hurt and it won't pain,
So it won't sting and it won't stain.

But it did.

Stamped: RETURN TO SENDER and nothing has changed.
The first dose of healing didn't take...
But they promise to baptize you
Like new.
They promise to humiliate you into not acting like this and not
Acting like that -

You say it's working this time and you tell me over and over why...
this time is not the same and now you understand.

I might as well have been speaking French and writing Braille.
I should have communicated in Swahili and been diagnosed illiterate.
I should have whispered into a disconnected and unplugged phone.
That's how much you understood.

But I don't.

It is now.
Only now.
When a blast of biology blessed
a miracle within us?

Was it my lack of tolerance in this recurring role
that sent me into considering alternatives
and kept me reaching for those few scarce moments
during the month
when a space like odyssey can occur?

Anti-biotics. Amoxicillin.
I just wanted to let go.
To ride with no hands.
To act like I didn't know.
I just wanted to not understand.

But I did.
I do.
I always have.

Hello Lover - Jacqueline Cioffa

She's there, standing right there in front of him
And the two steps forward separating their paths seem less heavy
And less likely to cross than the Brooklyn Bridge
In his steel toe Timberlands
Waiting by the curb, twiddling her restless fingers
Making fists inside her down coat pockets, and blowing frostbite smoke from her quivering lips
She's waiting
Again
For his piercing blue eyes, and messy brown scruff
To find their way
Back
Back to her
Back home around the bends
For him
To meet her on the corner for a late afternoon catch up
A latte, or cappuccino
Maybe they'd share a beer, it was almost quarter past noon
She didn't care either way
Conversation, she missed the first days and easy flirtations
The jitters, the half- dead lavender rose he handed her with a mischievous grin
The beginning days
Well, come on cross the street
Meet her less than halfway
He adjusted his scarf and collar, and looked directly into her eyes
Holding her gaze
Pulling down his skullcap, he turned away
He turned away
He turned and walked off

The daylight and black rims hid the tears she wiped quickly, absentmindedly from her face
Shocked, not shocked
Oh so typical
Oh God, not another one
She's been down and around the bends before
Not with him, perhaps
Perhaps she should've removed her shades
Blinders
But, oh there had been so many others
No different, no different at all
Messy brown boy replicas
One, two, three...and then four and five
Smiling through frozen tearsShe closed her eyes, and began to stitch up the heartache
With her steel fortress hardened mind
Reminiscing
Boots unable to move, feet frozen in subzero temperatures and time
There he was...
He was nice number three, or wait was he four?
His long brown, bleach blond curly hair, the carefree surfer dude with sunlight bouncing off his wet skin and toned abs
He made her fidgety, uncomfortable in her two-tone speedo and striped tan
He wasn't afraid of the depths she kept hidden or the mercurial ocean tidal pools of emotion
He wasn't put off by her weirdo ways, quirky ideas or razor sharp tongue
He didn't need to stand tall and puff out his chest
With his laid-back mind and chill temperament
She sat back in the sand, perched up on her elbows fully aware of his eyes on her back
Her dusk ombre shadow grew far from his as the sun descended slowly

That was okay
She didn't mind the distance
It would be dark soon, anyway
And they would wait together for the evening's stars
Sitting silent with the day's promise
And sand fights, dirty towels, flip flop giggles, tacos and cheap shot wine All in good fun banter
It was just right for a little while
She wasn't exactly unafraid, unsure of the man boy
She was uncertain of the empty promises from the others
The exact types that came before
He would become a stitch eventually in her already broken heart
Dirty, brown boys
Her first broke her like a Wild Mustang
Broke her for all others
The oh so fancy honest to God Rock star
She loved him, swooned and crooned at seventeen
He was too famous and the biggest liar she'd met thus far
Seventeen was a lifetime ago of music men, and silly romantic love songs
The first of too many sad
Dirty, brown boys who would break her heart, smash it, stomp on it
Pimp her out to the band
Really?
For fuck's sake
She was lanolin pretty, sexy sweet and delicious
Innocent, strong, smart, loyal, independent, funny, tender and naïve
Standing on the bitter cold corner, in yet another delusional big city

Snot pouring from her nose without a tissue
She'd cried this scenario before
She looked around as the pedestrians rudely bumped into her
Taxis flew by, and the streetlight went yellow, then red, and green twenty times
The stitches in her raw and freshly torn open heart growing thick
They would become scar tissue on top of scar tissue
Hurting less now than they did way back when
She'd have to find another corner, an alternate route home, and a new and different favorite coffee shop
If a dirty, brown boy came through the next door she swore she wouldn't look up
Who was she kidding?
Her heart was already busted and her pride
Well, like a bee stinger removed it couldn't hurt any worse
Or any less
Around the bends
Timing, a little luck and new promise waited
Inside her black felt, fringe hipster purse
Buried beneath her favorite red lipstick, an old flip phone, her beat up leather wallet, kohl eyeliner, chewing gum, sticky notes and various crap was a teeny, tiny sewing kit
For mending
She kept close it over the years
Holding tight to needle and thread

The Affair – SA Smith

I sit in a chair, near the window.
The light shines in on me, but I don't feel its warmth.
I look around, silence is everywhere.
I am left alone in a big empty house.
You tell me to smile, but how can I smile?
Can't you see that I am in pieces?
A mere fragment of the woman I once was.

You came into my life like a whirlwind.
A smile so bright, an infectious laugh.
You treated me like a queen.
You even bought me a castle.
We grew. We flourished. We loved.
Life happened around us, time flew by.
The sun smiled upon us.

I took it for granted you would always be here.
That you would always be mine.

I wanted you.
I needed you.
I loved you.

Until you loved someone else.

Now I'm alone in the dark
No light.
No love.
No hope.
Only pieces of us.
Pieces of a life I once had.
Of a dream I once shared.
Of the trust I once treasured.
And of the promise you didn't keep.

One thought. One decision. One action - changed everything.

You say you're sorry. You say we'll try.
But I can't try. I can't live.
I can't be that person, smiling through the pain.
While the question continually runs through my mind,

"Will he do it again?"

My heart is broken.
My trust is gone.
My hope is lost.

Those pieces of me that you broke,
They don't magically go back together.

I am forever changed.
You changed me.

How. Could. You.

Drano Love- Rebecca Charlotte

If only you could drown the heart in Drano,
unclogging the feelings stuck in your chest.
Feelings that will never find words effective enough
for containment.
These words need not be heavy,
since the sensation of danger is a strength in and of itself.
But they need to be colorful,
colorful enough to flash a message,
Help me help me help me
blinking like the light bulbs encircling a starlet's dressing room
mirror.
While these shooting stars fly down to earth,
propelled by a chemical orbit,
your heart is overdosing on feelings.
Just as quiet.
Just as deadly.
Help me help me help me
It feels like when you swallow a twenty-milligram pill of
Ritalin
and the yellow circle gets stuck in your throat.
Binding you, like a ribbon around a ballerinas' foot.
But only for a second.

What Do I Do - Brianna Scott

He's just for now
to take up time
and when we kiss I can't close my eyes
when he holds me it's not like you do
oh how I miss every inch of you
when I look into his eyes
I don't feel how I used to
I can't help but wonder if it's all worth it
but I can't keep coming home
to this
an empty bed and two unread text messages
when I wake up I wish it was next to you
oh how I miss every part of you
but for now I guess this will do
when your kisses can't reach to the other side of the ocean
your cyber moans don't turn me on anymore
when the hot summer nights are finally over
bundled up in our winter clothes
I can't even remember the sound of your voice anymore
this is when I have to find someone to replace you
but I swear they can't keep us apart
we'll meet again we'll meet again
in another life, I'll see him again
but until then
I can't keep counting down the days
I'll just sit here and fucking rot away
I can't help but look for you in the empty spaces
is this really a true love wasted

Love. (Lost?) - Wendy C. Garfinkle

i remember you.
when first we met
i, barely more than a child
you, already touched by war.
two different worlds
converging.

you
overcame my shyness
with your admiration for
my writing skills.
we
talked and exchanged numbers.
though we lived in the same town,
rarely met face-to-face
hours would pass on the telephone.

i remember you
you said
i
ruined
you
for any other woman.
but you kept returning
to them.
and then you let
me
go
too easily.
(why didn't you fight for me
why didn't you tell me
then
how you felt?)

i
lost
you
again
years later
when i returned.

she
had ruined you
for any other woman
even me.
but we talked again
more now;
and just when i thought
there was hope for
us,
you
abruptly left
me
for
another.

Mexico - Elizabeth Regen

i searched for You in mexico,

hoping to see Your face -
so many people resembled You
i felt your spirit in this foreign place.

i hunted for Your eyes
drew a picture of Your smile -
explained away Your hands
sat on the roadside for a while.

i imagined we had been there
when we were young and knew no better -
i lied about us swimming there,
in waters during stormy weather.

voices sound like yours

only with an accent i didn't know -
they sounded like your grandfather
i hear it - but it was so long ago.

i searched for You in Mexico
except i was by myself -
and i carried just a backpack
and i spoke to no one else.

i found a place with postcards
and i filled it up with words -
i licked it. stamped it. and sent it.
hoping You would get it.

how absurd.

the world there is crowded and
populated and alone -
but if by chance i'd found You there
i would never have gone home.

so maybe sometime in mexico
You can meet me and we can talk -
like a dream or like a movie
we can laugh again and walk.

i pictured You in mexico
waiting for me to arrive -
i'm waiting here in mexico

i hope that i survive.

Without You by My Side — F.K. Jadoon

I look for you in the hidden dustiest corners of a colorless life.
And when I don't find you there,
I die a little more;
one breath, one heartbeat at a time...

I make my way through life
like a blind man seeking his way through darkness.
Crashing into things,
getting bruised by falling onto glass-sprinkled ground,
hands bloodied by getting scraped,
body aching from the struggle...

Without you by my side,
life is nothing more than a deep, dark, drowning dungeon of despair.

Without you by my side,
life is a horrifying nightmare
from which I can never make myself escape.

Without you by my side,
I am a soul-less body seeking its host,
not knowing where to look.

Without you by my side,
I am a lost creature mourning the loss of its true mate.

Without you by my side,
I am a tormented wolf howling deep into the night,
calling out for his unrequited love to the moon.

Without you by my side,
I cease to exist and slowly fade into nothingness.

Without you by my side,
my mornings don't shine and the nights never end.

Peace by Piece – Nicole Lyons

It's during the moments when I'm quiet
that I foolishly give in to the idea
of peace.
I should know better
by now.
With every blow you laid
on me, you stripped me
of any chance
of peace
that I could have hoped for.
Now the bruises
have healed,
the scars blended
into shades
of me,
faded into almost
gone...almost.
The almost is what kills me
again,
taunts me and tells me what a coward I was.
It's the almost,
the faded pieces
that bring
up everything I never did,
every single thing
I never said.
Unspoken fears rise up
and curdle
against my tongue.

They threaten
to choke me.
So I swallow them,
again,
every last word
I never said to you,
and the burn
explodes through my body,

shredding it
piece by piece,
promising a life
without
peace,
if they go
unsaid
once more.

Listening Tears - Julie Anderson

Do *you* hear me? He asked.
Repeat what I just said.
No no no you have got it wrong
What the fuck is wrong with your head?
This isn't back then.
I used to scream with rage and belittle you, but not anymore.
I was just angry because I know you were playing dead.

No that's not it that is not what I said.

Why can't you see that you are a BITCH when it comes to me?
You are the one who is angry.
I am tired of your excuses.
Can't you hear the whispers behind your back?

Everyone knows that you are the one that is the mental case.
They tell me when I am alone.
They tell me what you said.
They tell me what you think.
They feel sorry for me that I have to put up with you.

You should just go and find another dream.
That is your problem, you are never satisfied.
Depression? *Oh please.*

Did you hear me?
Stop interrupting my thoughts.

I am trying to tell you that *you* are lucky to be loved.

It's not my problem it is yours.
You say that you don't know how,
 to share the feelings in your heart.
What the fuck is your problem?
Have you gone deaf?
I will tell you how it has been since that day you went sick.
It has been a struggle, to see you like this.

Get over it.
Stop talking about it.

I was sad then
Lonely for sure, that is because you just stopped participating in life.
That was it, a wall went up.

You left, you went deep into your head.
Your mind is playing tricks on you again.
I did not say that.
Why would I say something so cruel?
This is a nightmare.
Why are you so miserable to be around?

I keep telling you that all I want is you, I have never asked for more.
Ah, maybe you are just too stupid to see.
You have gone deaf dumb and mad on me.
Your frustrations are your own.

Live in the moment and let the rest go.
That was then, this is now.
I love you.

Did you hear what I just said?

Stop pretending to play like you are dead.
Respond dammit.
Say something.
Tell me that I am wrong.
The problem is yours.
It is not mine.

You are so fucked in the head

It is not my fault.
I did nothing wrong.
It is because of your past and the things that you did.
That is why I think you are so fucking filled with despair.

Grow up. You are not a kid anymore.
You should have followed your heart and tried those things back when you could.

Get out of your mind.
Do something more than just sit there and mourn.
Nobody gets to do want they want to do.
Why should *you* be any different?

That was then, this is now.

You are old. It is time to move on.
Deal with the fact that this is your life and you are the lucky one in the room.
You are too stupid to listen to me, you think that you can still chase after that wish.
Too stubborn to follow my lead, your ideas are beginning to reek.
The stench is killing me.

Stop saying that you can do this alone.
You will not survive without me I am sure.
No one has ever loved you like I do.

Listen. This is it.
One more word from you and I am out of here for good.
Are you there?

Did you hear what I just said?

Yes. I said.

I hear you.
I heard every word.
Look at my face.

Can't you see?

There Was - Ericka Arthur

There was an emptiness in your eyes that recoiled when called by name.
Shrinking at the mere thought of having to give me more.
More contact.
More answers.
Any more of you.
It was obvious that I had become painful to look at,
let alone love another day.

There was a part of me whose arms grew weary with each unresponsive touch; reaching habitually for familiar territory.
Wanting to believe I could not be that repulsive.
Certainly there was something in me that wooed the inner you.
I withdrew, craving what only you should be giving me;
weakened by every advance beckoning me across crowded empty rooms.

You wouldn't hold me and you wouldn't let me go.

I lingered,
not in denial but by happenstance.
Still, rising waters reminding me that I was wanted by someone(s),
somewhere else.
My meeting the unspoken needs of others,
without effort or mal-intent forever drained me.
It still does.

This Mask I Wear - SA Smith

I see the morning light coming through the window.
I roll over, not wanting to get up.
Not wanting to face another day,
just like the last.
How do I go on?
Why do I go on?

Everyone seems to be fine, seems to be moving forward.
But I'm not.
I am alone,
I have chosen it to be that way.

I don't want to share stories,
I don't want to listen to their small talk.
I want to be whole. I want to feel alive. I want to care again.
I want to be *me*.

The Me that could laugh,
feel the sun on her face and enjoy the enchantment of life.
But I'm not,
I don't even know who that person is anymore.

How was I ever her?
How did I ever live like that...
maybe I never did.
Maybe it was a mask that I unknowingly
threw on for the world,
preparing myself for now...
my new reality.

But now there is no mask,
now there is only me.

The uncertain smile I present to the world.
The world that doesn't want to see my cracks,
my fissures,
my emotional imperfections,
or the pain on my broken,
tear stained face.

"Be a good girl and smile. You don't look pretty when you're sad"

Hide it away they tell me.
Ignore it,
try to be happy.
But what do they know about me?
About walking in my shoes?

They only know what I've shown them,
what I've allowed them to see.

So again I will fake it.
I will smile and go through my day.

Hoping my new mask doesn't slip
Hoping that maybe tomorrow is the day it all changes.
Hoping that I can somehow learn-
to be the person I was before.

Before the darkness.
Before I lost me.

I Am a Woman - Katherine Grudens

Don't tell me I am too emotional to handle.
Don't tell me you love me just because you love my love handles.

Actually,
don't ever call them love handles.

My body was not made for you to hold on to.
Grab onto.
Pound into.
If my body is all you want to handle,
then you don't have respect for women.

I am a woman.

Don't tell me I am too needy to handle.
Don't tell me you like it better when I'm independent,
then get mad at me for not texting you back,
right away.

Actually,
don't tell me you like it better when I do anything.

Do you realize that just because you like something,
doesn't mean I am going to do it?

Silly boy.
I don't change my life for you.

I am a woman.

Don't tell me I am too fake for you to handle.
Don't tell me I am fake at all.

Actually,
don't ever use that word to describe a woman.

You say you like a girl natural,
but say I'm lazy when I have no makeup on.
Lazy when my hair isn't done.
Lazy when I'm comfortable in my own sweats.
In my own skin.
In my own body of a woman.

I am a woman.

I am not better than you.
I am not worse than you.
Yet you still can't settle on being,
equals.

Why is that?

Fools - Rachel Thompson

It bothered him I had secrets he knew about, and even more he didn't.

He wasn't the one, after all those many years, I felt like giving my secrets virginity to, scorching his ego more than how I secretly laughed at, and loathed, his thirty-second erections.

I am the fool, because I stay. It is enough.

Treating me that way, the only way he knows but doesn't see, twisting his thorny truths to fit flat in his palm of lies.

I am the fool because he stays. He is enough.

No, I don't want to listen anymore! I can't hear what will happen, what might change, meaningless letters dripping from his tongue, digging into my skin. Decades of faith lost inside my bones, I gasp at the sharp, messy realization of my mistake.

I loved him. Something so simple becomes so terribly complicated. I believed in him, and then I didn't. Left to right, right to left, up and down, down and up, marching marching marching through endless days. Opposites attract until they collide and atoms smash, leaving behind an explosive mess of ashes and pain.

But we didn't explode. It was more a quiet implosive retreat, patiently gathering my forces and wits, strategically placing every moment on my hidden board of fools, waiting, biding, holding each breath, pushing down every bitter verbal volley until I could finally, finally say it: leave.

I don't want your noise
your clutter
your patronizing cuts
your condescension
your hands that touch me without feeling
your eyes that don't see
your ears that don't hear
your mouth that interrupts
your arms that don't fold me in
your lies you believe
your lies you can't see
your lies you don't hear
your stories that have become so real to you
you don't even realize they never happened

your lies
your lies
your lies.

These were the secrets I held, and still hold, not for him, not against him, not because of him. No matter how long we are with one partner, we still have a secret inner life, desires that sustain us, folded up like paper hearts hidden in the deepest pockets of our souls. We fear the unfolding for what it will show, the razing it may cause, the cozy veneer of lies it burns away.

Fooling myself no longer.

I am enough.

Vile – Elizabeth Regen

i would rip your throat out
i would burn you to pieces
i'd leave you as ashes and never look back.
the collapse of your soul is
inevitable-
and everything you do is despicable.
there's nothing good
there's nothing clean
in how you're so mean
and i wish you death
YES! - with every breath i take i hope
the mistakes that you make pile up against you like rubble
and tumble upon you like snakes
you're a disgrace...
your poor mother.
your just another problematic personality in a society of
systematic bullshit and red tape.
i wish i could escape the sight of you - the thought
of your disappearance is excitable-
behind your desk- proud of your power.
get in the shower and wash yourself fully-
you're a bully and made of dust...
you'll never matter- especially to us.

The Anatomy of a Breakup - Valeria Vaughn

Panic flight illuminated by lines of city street lights cries out in the night,
gunned down, violent massacres an anchor weight around society's neck.
Controlled chaos - a death here and death there, no one really stops to stare,
not for too long these days.
Own to an "It could have been me mentality."
Party lines argue who's to blame, but it's never their name taking the blame.
Around we go again, either fall in line
or get left behind, or some that say,
those left as prisoners
to feel the pain of the mundane money-worship workdays
five days within each week
this rule of thumb crush under-paid slavery.

Life will be fine a mother's soft, assuring voice sings a lullaby to a small child
cradled in her protective arms,
as bombs rain down tears of sadness full of despair.
Death clinches chests full of lifeless air washed ashore
in an unforgiving world,
moisten steps of tears weep for a small child,
swept away by fear and intolerance
a body left lifeless by destruction of hope and humanity.

On the front lines of our public execution, bare minimum-wage earners on a path
to poverty made workers rising at the sun's shine to make
a few bucks and a dime selling our time to the world of corporate slavery
the glimpse of the crossfire hair aimed towards dissection in a unison direction.
The other side of madness that damn feeling of anxiety
rears its ugly head once again,
as coins get us to the next payday.

What feels like a global crash crushes the soul, yet the heart will always remain
the fool.
Redemption only a smile away to brush back the curtains which protect us from the day's fear.

Shall we weep upon this very stage?
Built from wooden planks made of tongue-n-groove, side-by-side,
fit so perfectly together, come together a shelter from the shit storm of life,
mostly without reason - moods change such as the seasons, growth of shelter
blooms in the spring.
Trees grow timber to set yet another stage.

Up next, the same old mess.
The first step away from the crash is always the hardest first step to take
as heads fill with confusion, spin without direction
a much-sought-after lucidity, like swarms of bees we drop to our knees
in utter disgust at the trivial pursuit of material things.
A cursor of a person defined by marginal abilities, conformist miss the mark
reaching out for a warm body in the dark.

Outstretched, bone-thin, hungry hands guide a panicked heart's reality,
clawing for anything to hold as transparency begins to slow the memories
of past forgotten affairs.

Broken will, a fixable flaw
in the construction wheel of life engaged with awaken-eyes,
no longer blind due to deception and lies,
as another hello ends in goodbye.

The Taste of Your Absence - Darla Halyk

I taste the dirt you left in my mouth
Infected with injury, grit-stained teeth
You lied, and I purchased each facade
Opening my aching, needy soul
Turning my words into blood, for the devil

Don't call me baby, or girl
Your ego needed me to feel complete
And while I patched my heart to yours
With a needle and tainted thread
I turned into garbage, a waste of your time

You reached inside my rib cage
Removed my heart, abandoned it
Haphazardly dropping it into shreds of insecurity
You understood the reservation it contained
Releasing my bloodied breast to the wolves

It can't have been authentic
Forgotten so quick, tossed away
Sincerity lost, rocks thrown, blame placed
It wasn't me installing lies in your ears
For you were the one unable to believe

My heart contained a need for completion
Unitedness I was willing to provide unrestricted
For my heart, sensed you, consumed you
Starved to be all you demanded
Now my spirit is lost, forgotten.

And as the blood seeps to the surface
My tired skin, missing your touch
I feel more bruised than broken
More sadness than anger
More regret than tears

Last Night I Dreamt Somebody Loved Me - Stephanie Ortez

This story is old, but it goes on.
Last night she dreamt somebody loved her,
The walls she built came tumbling down,
One by one
Her chains were broken,
Revealing this famine heart aching to be free
If only he could see all she wants is to be adored.

She is falling before his eyes
Is even worth it?
Something so precious must serve a purpose
This feeling of urgency,
When time stays still,
waiting anxiously until the night comes soon.
She wants to see beauty, she wants to see life.
Why does she give her time if she knows he doesn't care if she cries or laughs?
Seeking love in the wrong places,
seeking love in so many faces.
She doesn't want to wake up on her own anymore.
Last night she dreamt somebody loved her;
The white wedding dress, the memories, and pictures
She knows it's over.
This story is old, but it goes on.
She wants the one she can't have.

White Picket Fence – Julie Anderson

Material possessions are worth nothing.
It is love and family that counts for everything.

Before the after, I tried to have it all.
Long days added up to years of lonely rambling,
came to a stop when I found my first true love.

He was it.
He was special.
He was my life.

I gave up on international adventures,
I gave up contracts,
I gave up on being alone.

We were a family.
He and I,
my son,
a Labrador puppy,
convertible Cadillac,
VIP pass to the stars.

What I thought was the beginning of life ever after,
never took off.
That kind of life was not meant for him; Peter Pan is forever young.
I was a wild card.
Gamblers, the best ones, don't bet on the likes of me.

I packed,
moved my son,
left everything behind.
The next day.

The house was white.
It sat back from traffic,
elevated just enough,
so that I could pretend that it was a fortress on the hill.
It was a beauty in the old victorian section of my hometown.

Oak trees swayed, Spanish moss dangled.
Azaleas bloomed, leaves fell, the dogs barked.
Large enough for all,
it remained cavernous,
echoes of two.

Then there was the boyfriend from Prague; he left patience.
Then there was the boyfriend from Pennsylvania; he left
passion and an unborn child.
Then there was the boyfriend from Texas; he left diamonds,
paranoia, and a tax audit.

Christmas came,
the ex-husband stayed over.
He watched his son,
pathetic fake fatherly pride.
The wolf ate the ham,
Gifts ripped apart.

Always alone,
I stuffed the atmosphere with
animals,
toys,
furniture,
books,
chaos, and adventure.
Always empty,
even though I dreamed,
wished,
prayed for a home,
stability and safety would be the delicious side effects.

We married in the backyard.
Roses red,
filled vases that were lit by a thousand candles.
The uncles were drunk.
Cigars smoked.

The house caught on fire.
The best wedding ever.
The only wedding I know of that never had a honeymoon.

A daughter was born,
greeted by my grandmother,
adored by my mom,
celebrated by all.

She was ferried out of the hospital as if she would break.

The most fragile of miracles.
That was when eyes and mouths planned,
schemed,
organized a proper nanny.
The verdict always delivered with a knife, right in my back.

We left the house perched on the hill,
that slept under the oaks,
decorated with azaleas,
gardenias and hibiscus,
one week later.

I was told,
the sheets were not good enough.
Bought at Target,
the thread count was shit,
not even made from cotton.
I was told,
my other child was spoiled,
that I was not a proper parent,
my house needed order.
I was told,
that we could not stay,
we had to move to chase the dollar.

The house had a white picket fence.
That fence evoked sarcastic laughter,
a period at the end of the
"she is out of her mind" declaration.
The house sat empty for a year.
It's windows dark, the sparkle of life gone; it was alone.

Alone. Under the trees. Sparkling pool, sun shining. Alone.

I tried to go home. I tried to make a home. I tried.

It was not good enough.

Years later,
memories still turned over and examined.
Laughter, then heartbreak.
That was the middle time.

The white picket fence was torn down by the new owners.
The French doors ripped off and thrown to the curb.
The trees still stand,
so does the house.

I can't and won't drive by.
It hurts,
to see.
It hurts to remember.
For me, the house represents what could have been.

I am told to let the past go.
I find that I can't forget heartbreak.

Just Fine - Rachel Thompson

I'm not who you want me to be, and that's fine.

No, it's not fine.
Fine is fucked. Fuck you, fine.
Fine means cool, copacetic, mellow.
You think that's what it means to be me.

I am hot,
I am not in excellent order,
I am tired,
Of you telling me what to do,
How to feel,
What to think,
How to be.
I am not your mother's daughter.
I am me.

I brazenly sashay my swinging hips,
Up to your delicious mouth,
Dripping with their coarse demands,
Chewing your thick, cherry lips,
Tearing your lost mumblings,
As red drips from my gnashing teeth.
Who owns your wants now?

This tough girl who used to quietly shrink at your words.
My heart shoves hard at my chest, wanting out.
Tears form and fall as I wipe them away with a furious fist.
Hating to admit how much it hurts,
When you shred me.

Why do you think what you say matters?
Stunning, how the breeze flows without your say.
Pebbles may move in your wake,
But never trees.

This is my life, and you have no access key.
I don't want to be fine in your eyes, whatever that is.
Talk to yourself with your bloody mouth full of ire.
Go be fine in your own life.

I want more.
I want free.

AUTHOR BIOGRAPHIES

Julie Anderson:

Julie is the creator and publisher of Feminine Collective. Formerly known at the "face" for many luxury brands during her reign as a 90's Supermodel. She has lived and worked on six continents and has always been eager to learn more about the lives of all the individuals that she encounters. After twenty plus years on the road, she considers herself extremely lucky to have found her "voice." As a writer and poet, she uses her platform as part therapy and part recreation of what it means to be comfortable in her skin. An avid amateur photographer, many of her photographs can be found on femininecollectiv.com. The community of writers that has been cultivated on Feminine Collective and their work has brought peace and meaning to her life. She is a mental health advocate and is the managing director of the LifeAfter Project Inc., a nonprofit organization that provides educational content designed to inspire and spread awareness for suicide prevention, substance abuse and domestic abuse on a global scale. Julie is the proud mother of three wildly unique children, which she loves madly, even though they drive her insane. To find out more visit julieandersonofficial.com. Her column, "Pursuit of Perfection" can be found on femininecollective.com. Connect on Twitter: @1JULIEANDERSON

S.A. Smith:

Besides being a bestselling author of a four book Paranormal Romance book series, she is also a partner and columnist at Feminine Collective. SA uses her writing to be an advocate for women of all shapes and sizes. Believing that we are all enough just as we are, and needing to spread that word far and wide. Having been diagnosed with CRPS over 12 years ago, SA also uses her writing to increase social awareness of other Invisible Illnesses. To find out more about SA's books or writings, visit her website at AuthorSASmith.com. Her column, "Love Bytes" can be found on femininecollective.com. Connect on Twitter: @SherriAnnSmith

Stephanie Ortez:

Stephanie claims that 99% of the time her brain is thinking about her kids, blah, meh, why, huh, WTF, her dog and writing. The other 1% works as an admissions advisor for the International Academy, and George Washington University High School Online. She is a mental health advocate and activist. Her column, "El Rincon de Stephanie" can be found on femininecollective.com. Connect on Twitter: @StephyOrtez

John Michael Antonio:

Editor and columnist at Feminine Collective. John is also freelance writer and photographer. He has been married to his wife, the love of his life, for nearly thirty years and is the father of three wonderful children. His column, "Inside Man" can be found on femininecollective.com. Connect on Twitter: @tigermichael100

Jacqueline Cioffa:

Feminist. Mental Health Advocate. Poet. Activist. Dog Lover. Model. Celebrity Make Up Artist. Stone Crab Enthusiast. Humanitarian. The author of the poignant soul-stirring saga, "The Vast Landscape" and "Georgia Pine." Jacqueline's work has also been widely featured in numerous literary magazines and anthologies. She's a storyteller, observer, truth teller, essayist, potty mouth and film lover who's traveled the world. She believes passionately in using her voice to advocate, help and inspire others. Her column, "Bleeding Ink" can be found on femininecollective.com. Visit jacquelinecioffa.com, to find out more about her writing and books. Connect on Twitter: @JackieCioffa

Richard De Fino:

Richard is a non-fiction writer and poet born and raised in New York City. He currently resides in Buffalo New York with his wife, two cats, and dog. His column, "The Anxiety Monologues" can be found on femininecollective.com. Connect on Twitter: @rickydefino

Nicole Lyons:

Nicole is a poet, with a hippie's heart and a bohemian soul, who believes that the world can be changed by one random act of kindness at a time. She writes her poetry from beautiful British Columbia where she advocates for mental health and volunteers as a speaker and event coordinator with a Canadian NPO that focuses on suicide prevention in children and teens. Her column, "Between Memories and Scars" can be found on femininecollective.com. Visit thelithiumchronicles.org to find out more about her writing and poetry. Connect on Twitter: @LithChronicles

Dori Owen:

Dori is a storyteller. She shares her tales as a Feminine Collective columnist. She writes from small town Arizona where she grew up, after living a few decades in California as an LA Wild Child. Her column, "Diary of an Arizona Girl" can be found on femininecollective.com. Connect on Twitter: @doriowen

Dave Pacailler:

After living under a rock for nearly 25 years, Dave had his eyes opened wide to the world in 2010 after marrying his crazy cat lady wife. Officially straight, but defined by some as metro, you will typically find him cleaning the house instead of working out in the yard. In his spare time, Dave enjoys playing the guitar and writing sappy love songs. Living in Florida, he endures a comedic life with his wife, teenage stepdaughter, five cats and a dog that no one likes. His column, "A Wave of Dave" can be found on femininecollective.com. Connect on Twitter: @AWaveOfDave

Elizabeth Regen:

The mother of 3 beautiful girls, Elizabeth is actively fighting to leave them a better world. Her column, "The Way I See It" can be found on femininecollective.com. Connect on Twitter: @ElizabethRegen

Natasha Alexander: Always a wife and mother first, Natasha is flawed yet loved. Now she knows that she does not have to chase perfection. Instead, she chases her dreams. Connect on Twitter: @NatashaKledAlex

Ericka Arthur: Ericka is known as a fearless writer behind the pen. A Brooklyn, NY native, Ericka is an Inspirational Blogger, speaker, writer, singer, and poet. She is a lover of love, she writes from the core of the heart to the core of the heart. Connect on Twitter: @authenticitee

Margret Avery: Margret has always written poetry and would hide it in drawers all over her apartment. Then one day she chose to share them, and there is no going back. It never fails to intrigue her through the inspirations she has in her life to have a foray into this world of words that may touch another person's life. Connect on Twitter: @MargretAvery

Paakhi Bhatnagar: Paakhi is a high school student from India, a fiery feminist, and a passionate writer and blogger. She writes for her local newspaper, The Gulf News, and her works have been published on Feminine Collective, Stigma Fighters, Urbanette, Off the Coast, and Canvas Literary Journal. Connect on Twitter: @paakhi13

Susan P. Blevins: Susan was born in England. She lived twenty-six wonderful years in Italy, where she wrote a weekly column for an international newspaper. She then spent fourteen years in New Mexico, writing about gardens and gardening. Now Susan calls Houston, Texas home. Her essays, fiction, and poetry have been published in various literary forums. All of her work is based on her travels, adventurous life and philosophy. She knows now with absolute certainty that the only things that matter in life are love and service, and to that end, she hopes to spread light and love to everyone she meets, one smile, one laugh, and one hug at a time. She believes that we are one.

Nan Byrne: Nan is a poet and television writer. She is the author of two books, and her stories and poems have appeared in a variety of literary magazines including Michigan Quarterly Review, Seattle Review, Canadian Woman Studies, Fiction Southeast, and elsewhere. She is currently working on a forthcoming novel. Connect on Twitter: @heatspell

Lela Casey: A seeker of wisdom Lela is always on the look out for adventures and kindred spirits. You can find her writing on many websites including femininecollective.com, Kveller.com, thewisdomdaily.com and brainchildmag.com

Natalie N. Caro: Bronx-born educator & writer, Natalie used to want to be a mermaid. But she learned to write before she learned to swim. Connect on Twitter: @scatteredstanza

Rebecca Charlotte: Rebecca spends her days working on getting her Masters in Library and Information Science from Simmons College and her nights watching superhero shows and writing poetry. Her work has appeared in the Feminine Collective, BUST, elephant journal, and Her Campus. Connect on Twitter: @becca_writes

Rachael Convery: Maker, scholar, and wearer of many hats, Rachael considers her life's work to be the constant pursuit of beauty. Rachael hails from the small and curious isle of Martha's Vineyard, though her gypsy wagon is currently berthed in the fabulous southern metropolis of New Orleans, which she is thrilled to once again make her home with her small apricot-and-white cat and an ever-expanding collection of books. Connect on Twitter: @alternatiVe_mv

Sandy Coomer: A poet and mixed media artist from Nashville, TN, Sandy is the author of three poetry chapbooks, including the forthcoming, "Rivers Within Us" (Unsolicited Press).

Kelley Cooper: Kelley is a life coach who guides women to connect with every part of who they are. She serves as a guide through the personal transformation journey of finding your inner wise woman. Through her live events, she creates space for women to play, connect, inspire one another, and heal. Kelley lives in Lake Tahoe, CA, with her husband and dog, Huey. Her happy place is deep in the forest among the trees and river.

Wendy C. Garfinkle: Over-educated editor and writer, Wendy is an avid reader and traveler, who loves caffeine, storms and dark chocolate. She works in law enforcement and lives in South Florida with her teenage son. Connect on Twitter: @wendygarfinkle

Megan Garner: Writer, gamer, and foodie, Megan is a happy resident of Orange, CA. She lives with her loving wife and old cat. Professionally, she works as a content marketing specialist, though her writer's heart prefers to sing out in poetry, fantasy novels, and comedic screenplays.

Katherine Grudens: A recent graduate of Ithaca College, Katherine has always turned to writing to help express what she is going through, especially now as she tries to adjust to life back at home on Long Island. She aspires to bring light and truth into everything she creates and is dedicated to carrying that mission with her both in her personal and professional life. Connect on Twitter: @KGrudens

HastyWords: Anxiety driven over-analyzer with a mind full of rainbows and devils, HastyWords began writing poetry to give her tears and laughter a voice. Connect on Twitter: @HastyWords

Darla Halyk: Darla is the mother of a teenage boy and girl. She is a lover of verbal irony, which currently drives her two children insane. You can find her writing on the Elephant Journal, Sammiches and Psyche Meds, Mrs.Muffin Top, BLUNTmoms, Scary Mommy, Original Bunker Punks. She has also been featured on Blogher. She is a regular contributor and Editor to The Soap Box and currently writes for her blog at NewWorldMom.com. She brings a fresh, honest and humorous take on parenting, women's issues, relationships, divorce, and life in general. Connect on Twitter: @newworldmoms

Clementine Heath: Clementine is an accomplished actress and writer for TV and film in Hollywood. She began writing poetry in her teens as a personal hobby until she started sharing her work with Feminine Collective in 2016.

Tennessee Hill: Tennessee is currently a sophomore at Stephen F. Austin State University working toward her BFA in Creative Writing. She is an alum of The Sewanee Young Writers' Conference. Her work has been featured in The Sandy River Review, Elle Journal, Kaaterskill Basin, HUMID and Feminine Collective. Connect on Twitter: @Tenny_Elizabeth

F.K. Jadoon: A native of Pakistan, English is F.K. Jadoon's second language. She writes to find a voice in this over-crowded, over-critical and over-judgemental world. She is a great admirer of words and can't help falling under their spell when she encounters them on dark, lonely nights. She says that she exorcises her demons by writing about them in ink. Connect on Twitter: @fk_jadoon741

H.M. Jones: Award-winning author of fantasy, sci-fi, and poetry, H.M. Jones is also a burgeoning illustrator and avid blogger. In her spare time, she wrangles two kids, three chickens, one cat and one silly mutt. Find her at hmjones.net. Connect on Twitter: @HMJonesWrites.

Veronica Mattaboni: Veronica is a poetry and fiction writer from Pennsylvania. She graduated from West Chester University with a B.A. in English and a minor in Creative Writing. Connect on Twitter: @whatdarkpasages

Peter M. Olsen: After graduating from Washington State University with a B.A. in Humanities, Peter found his real passion as a blogger at razorcast.net. He is a raver, PLUR warrior, video game junkie, coffee addict and an all-around pretty cool guy. Peter lives in the greatest city on Earth, the Emerald City, Seattle, Washington. Connect on Twitter: @banishedcougar

Jessica Rinker: Earned her MFA from Vermont College of Fine Arts and is a children's author, freelance writer, and editor. She lives in New Jersey with her partner, Joe, who is also an author and pulls endless inspiration from their kids and long walks along the Delaware River. Connect of Twitter: @jm_rinker

Kim Sisto Robinson: A lover of beautiful words and an advocate for all women, Kim created her blog, My Inner Chick, to honor of her sister, after her husband murdered her in 2010. Connect on Twitter: @krrobi

Icess Fernandez Rojas: Icess is an Afro-Latina writer and teacher from Houston. She is a VONA alum and has an MFA from Goddard College. Check out her blog at icessfernandez.com. Connect on Twitter: @Icess

Brianna Scott: Writer, avid explorer, Brianna is also a hopeless romantic. She lives in Northern California and is currently a student at UC Davis. Connect on Twitter: @Brianna_jpg

Tabitha Stirling: Writer and poet from Edinburgh, Scotland, Tabitha's publishing credits include Mslexia, Feminine Collective, Literary Orphans and Twisted Sister. Loss, grief, mental illness, strength, and love are recurring themes in both her poetry and fiction. Connect on Twitter: @VoleQueen

C. Streetlights: C. Streetlights grew up, as people do, earned a few degrees and became a teacher. She spent her days discussing topics like essay writing, Romeo, and Juliet, the difference between a paragraph and a sentence. She has met many fools but admires Don Quixote most because he taught her that it didn't matter that the dragon turned out to be a windmill. What mattered was that he chose to fight the dragon in the first place. She now lives in the mountains with a husband, two miracle children, and a dog who eats Kleenex. She retired from teaching so she can raise her children to pick up their underwear from the bathroom floor, to write, and to slay windmills and dragons. She is the author of "Tea and Madness" and the recently published memoir "Black Sheep Rising," both books are available on Amazon. Connect on Twitter: @CStreetlights

Rachel Thompson: Rachel is an author, advocate, survivor of childhood sexual abuse, business owner, and is a happy single mom. She released the "BadRedHead Media 30-Day Book Marketing Challenge" in December 2016 to rave reviews. She is the author of the award-winning, bestselling "Broken Places" (one of the IndieReader's "Best of 2015" top books and 2015 Honorable Mention Winner in both the Los Angeles and San Francisco Book Festivals. She is also the author of the bestselling, multi-award-winning "Broken Pieces." Find her on RachelintheOC.com or Amazon worldwide. Connect on Twitter: @RachelintheOC

Valerie Vaughn: American poet and short story writer, Valerie was the 2015 Editor's Pick Recipient. She received her Bachelors of Arts in History from Mary Baldwin University. Connect on Twitter: @ValerieRVaughn

Tiffani Burnett-Velez: Tiffani's articles and essays have appeared in Pennsylvania Magazine, Yahoo!News and other magazines in the US and Europe. Her prose has been published in Toe Good Poetry and Feminine Collective. She is the author of three Amazon bestselling novels. She lives in Pennsylvania with her family. Connect on Twitter: @tiffanibvelez

Elizabeth Kirkpatrick Vrenios: Music Professor Emerita from American University, Elizabeth was recently featured in Tupelo Press's 30/30 challenge and has been published in many online and printed publications. Her chapbook "Special Delivery," written about the Pan Am 103 Crash was a Yellow Chair Press prize winner. Published in 2016 it is available for purchase on Amazon.

Catherine Zickgraf: Catherine has the distinction of performing her poetry in Madrid, San Juan, and three dozen other cities around the world. Her recent chapbook, "Soul Full of Eye" (Aldrich Press) is available on Amazon.

Love Notes From Humanity

We hope you enjoyed:

LOVE NOTES FROM HUMANITY

THE LUST, LOVE & LOST COLLECTION

Come Visit Us At
FeminineCollective.com

For More Like-Minded

Articles & Poetry

Poem Copyrights:
"Phantom Heart" "Daughter" "Seductress of Sin" "Sex With Strangers" "Listening Tears" "UnLovAble" "While You Were Away" "Carnal Dream" "White Picket Fence" by Julie Anderson. Copyright © 2015-2016 Julie Anderson. Reprinted by permission of the author.
"Hero" "No Wonder" "Beautiful Cage" by Natasha Alexander. Copyright © 2016 Natasha Alexander. Reprinted by permission of the author.
"Morning Glory" "Promises in the Dark" "The Revealing" "Dreams" "Guilty Pleasures" "Why Men Secretly Fear Women" by John Michael Antonio. Copyright © 2016-2017 John Michael Antonio. Reprinted by permission of the author.
"There Was" by Ericka Arthur. Copyright © 2016 Ericka Arthur. Reprinted by permission of the author.
"An Abyss" "Turn the Page" by Margret Avery. Copyright © 2015-2016 Margret Avery. Reprinted by permission of the author.
"Presence in Absence" by Paakhi Bhatnagar. Copyright © 2016 Paakhi Bhatnagar. Reprinted by permission of the author.
"Gardening Tip" "Apparitions" by Susan P. Blevins. Copyright @ 2016 Susan P. Blevins. Reprinted by permission of the author.
"Chapin Street" by Nan Byrne. Copyright © 2016 Nan Byrne. Reprinted by permission of the author.
"My Heart Tastes Like Chicken" by Lela Casey. Copyright © 2016 Lela Casey. Reprinted by permission of the author.
"Honesty" by Natalie Caro. Copyright © 2017 Natalie Caro. Reprinted by permission of the author.
"Drano Love" by Rebecca Charlotte. Copyright © 2016 Rebecca Charlotte. Reprinted by permission of the author.
"Sunflowers and Sticky Tape" "Love Stinks" "Hello Lover" by Jacqueline Cioffa. Copyright © 2016-2017 Jacqueline Cioffa. Reprinted by permission of the author.
"V.5" by Rachael Convery. Copyright © 2016 Rachael Convery. Reprinted by permission of the author.
"Once" "To Kiss a Married Man" by Sandy Coomer. Copyright © 2015-2016 Sandy Coomer. Reprinted by permission of the author.
"A Man I Used to Love" by Kelley Cooper. Copyright © 2015 Kelley Cooper. Reprinted by permission of the author.
"Romantics" by Richard DeFino. Copyright © 2016 Richard DeFino. Reprinted by permission of the author.
"Love (Lost?)" by Wendy C. Garfinkle. Copyright @ 2016 Wendy C. Garfinkle. Reprinted by permission of the author.
"The Ocean is a Woman" by Megan Garner. Copyright © 2016 Megan Garner. Reprinted by permission of the author.
"Parliaments" "I Am a Woman" by Katherine Grudens. Copyright © 2016 Katherine Grudens. Reprinted by permission of the author.
"Humanity" by Hasty Words. Copyright © 2016 Hasty Words. Reprinted by permission of the author.
"The Taste of Your Absence" by Darla Halyk. Copyright © 2016 Darla Halyk. Reprinted by permission of the author.
"Mistress Desire and The Lonely Flame" "The Descent" "Disintegration" "Absolution" by Clementine Heath. Copyright © 2016 Clementine Heath. Reprinted by permission of the author.
"F1 Generation" "Bergamot" by Tennessee Hill. Copyright © 2016 Tennessee Hill. Reprinted by permission of the author.

"My Addiction" "Transformation" "Without you by my Side" by F.K. Jadoon. Copyright @ 2016 F.K. Jadoon. Reprinted by permission of the author.

"Stuck Inside" by H.M. Jones. Copyright © 2016 H.M. Jones. Reprinted by permission of the author.

"How To Love A Wanderer "The Colour of Us" "Peace By Piece" "Evanescence "by Nicole Lyons. Copyright © 2016 Nicole Lyons. Reprinted by permission of the author.

"Perfect Girlfriend Learns the Word Normal" by Veronica Mattaboni. Copyright © 2016 Veronica Mattaboni. Reprinted by permission of the author.

"It Happened Under the Electric Sky" by Peter M. Olsen. Copyright © 2017 Peter M. Olsen. Reprinted by permission of the author.

"Unhappy Girl" "Last Night I Dreamt Somebody Loved Me" by Stephanie Ortez. Copyright © 2016 Stephanie Ortez. Reprinted by permission of the author.

"All I Ask" "Bad Things" "Someday Someway" by Dori Owen. Copyright © 2016 Dori Owen. Reprinted by permission of the author.

"Damaged Goods" by Dave Pacailler. Copyright © 2016 Dave Pacailler. Reprinted by permission of the author.

"House Keys" "High School Teen Age Dreams" "First Hours of Forever" "Mexico" "First Try" "Vile" by Elizabeth Regen. Copyright © 2014-2016 Elizabeth Regen. Reprinted by permission of the author.

"Eleven" by Jessica Rinker. Copyright © 2016 Jessica Rinker. Reprinted by permission of the author.

"You Rise" by Kim Sisto-Robinson. Copyright © 2016 Kim Sisto-Robinson. Reprinted by permission of the author.

"I Promise" by Icess Fernandez Rojas. Copyright © 2016 Icess Fernandez Rojas. Reprinted by permission of the author.

"What Do I Do" "The Skin I'm In, Loved and Lost" by Brianna Scott. Copyright © 2016 Brianna Scott. Reprinted by permission of the author.

"You Are Mine" "You Are Star Stuff" "The Affair" "Broken" "This Mask I Wear" by S.A. Smith. Copyright © 2016-2017 S.A. Smith. Reprinted by permission of the author.

"Bare Bones Of It" "Bi-Polar Love "by Tabitha Stirling. Copyright © 2016 Tabitha Stirling. Reprinted by permission of the author.

"Eden's Palpitation" "Playing For Keepsies" "And What of That Vortex" by C. Streetlights. Copyright © 2016-2017 C. Streetlights. Reprinted by permission of the author.

"Fools" "Elements on Fire" "Just Fine "by Rachel Thompson. Copyright © 2015-2017 Rachel Thompson. Reprinted by permission of the author.

"The Anatomy of a Breakup" by Valerie Vaughn. Copyright © 2016 Valerie Vaughn. Reprinted by permission of the author.

"Sapling" by Tiffani Velez. Copyright © 2016 Tiffani Velez. Reprinted by permission of the author.

"Every Other Thursday" "My Lover Does Not Deserve Black" by Elizabeth Kirkpatrick Vrenios. Copyright © 2016 Elizabeth Kirkpatrick Vrenios. Reprinted by permission of the author.

"What It Was Worth" by Catherine Zickgraf. Copyright © 2016 Catherine Zickgraf. Reprinted by permission of the author.

Made in the USA
Lexington, KY
18 February 2017